CIVICS 101

POEMS ABOUT AMERICA'S CITIES

ROGER L. KEMP

authorHOUSE

AuthorHouse™
1663 Liberty Drive
Bloomington, IN 47403
www.authorhouse.com
Phone: 833-262-8899

Published by AuthorHouse 02/23/2022

ISBN: 978-1-6655-5309-4 (sc)
ISBN: 978-1-6655-5310-0 (e)

Library of Congress Control Number: 2022903552

Print information available on the last page.

*Any people depicted in stock imagery provided by Getty Images are models,
and such images are being used for illustrative purposes only.
Certain stock imagery © Getty Images.*

This book is printed on acid-free paper.

DEDICATION

This book is dedicated to Kieran,
The best and the brightest

CONTENTS

Lesson 3: The Urban Scene

Lesson 4: The Government

Lesson 5: From the Trenches

Lesson 6: Personal Reflections

Lesson 7: Closing Thoughts

Lesson 8: The Future

ACKNOWLEDGEMENTS

Grateful acknowledgements are made to the elected officials, appointed officials, and citizens, of those cities that I have worked and lived in during my over a quarter-century public service career on both coasts of the United States.

These states and cities include the following:

- In California   –   The City of Oakland
                        The City of Seaside
                        The City of Placentia
                        The City of Vallejo

- In New Jersey   –   The City of Clifton

- In Connecticut   –   The City of Meriden
                        The Town of Berlin

PREFACE

Citizens generally have a desire to learn more about America's cities, including their own community's municipal government. This is true because people spend most of their lives living, working, and paying municipal taxes in cities. Many citizens, however, know more about their state and federal government, than they do about the city in which they live. This is primarily due to the extensive media coverage given to topical issues and news events, plus what they, as students, were never taught in high school civics classes many years ago.

City government is the level of government of which citizens should be most informed. After all, the decisions made by local elected public officials – mayors and city council members – have a more direct and greater impact on their lives than do those decisions made by elected leaders in higher levels of government. This thirst for knowledge is made apparent when speaking before community groups and professional organizations about how municipal government works. Most citizens want to know more about the operations of their local government, including the roles of their elected officials, advisory bodies, chief administrative officer, and the various functional managers that make government work.

It is a shame that most high school civics classes, while starting the semester with aggressive goals to educate students about all levels of government, end before reaching the level of government closest to the people – municipal government. The author remembers how quickly the semester ended, usually right after learning about two of the three levels of government. But typically, never covering cities and, if so, only briefly providing a nominal understanding at best. In the field of higher education, this topic is generally thought to be to elementary to be included in college-level classes. Hence, this work has been titled *Civics 101*.

For these reasons, the author has written a collection of poems based on a quarter-century of actual experience working in various communities, and his relationships with their elected officials and citizens. This experience was gained in politically, economically, and racially diversity communities on both the East and West Coasts over an entire life of public service. During his career, the author has served a dozen mayors, several city councils, and scores of local elected officials.

This collection of poems encompasses the author's childhood desire to visit cities, along with his twenty years of experience serving as an appointed municipal chief executive officer. To provide insights into the various facets of America's cities, this volume has been divided into seven sections, or lessons. Each lesson should provide the reader with an understanding and insight about a particular aspect of our cities. Together, they will give the reader a better understanding about our nation's cities, their politics, as well as how they function.

Lesson One provides a general overview of America's cities, ranging from the author's experience as a boy to his reflections as a seasoned chief executive officer in several cities. Lesson Two lends insight into local community politics and politicians, covering such topics as elections and employee unions. Lesson Three examines our urban landscape and environment, and the impact that seemingly unchecked urban growth has had on the fabric of our society.

Lesson Five is a compilation of actual war stories direct from the front-lines of battle in the local political arena over many years. Lesson Six offers personal reflections of the author about various aspects of cities based on numerous years working in them, as well as his travels to cities in other countries around the world. Generic titles, such as mayor and city council members, are used to protect the innocent as well as the guilty.

The concluding section, Lesson Seven, provides closing thoughts about our cities and how to improve their workings, and offers personal reflections of an aging, seasoned bureaucrat. Despite his 25-years' experience working in numerous communities, the author feels that any individual's knowledge of cities is somewhat limited. It is this writer's belief that, to truly get to know a city, you must actually live in it to experience its unique "flavor" first-hand.

These poems are a reflection of the experience gained and the battle scars received from over two decades of service as a city manager. This work should provide insight to citizens wishing to learn more about the workings of America's cities, or merely the operations of their own community's municipal government. Lastly, this volume will enhance the reader's understanding about cities in general – the place where they live and spend most of their lives.

The author hopes that readers enjoy these poems as much as he enjoyed writing them and preparing this volume. Without further ado, it's now time to turn to Lesson One! While there is no final examination at the end of these lessons, it is hoped that, after reading this book, citizens will become more astute in their deals with the public officials and bureaucrats at City Hall who run their community's government.

Roger L. Kemp

LESSON ONE

AMERICA'S CITIES

A Child's Dream

As a child, wondering about cities
I would visit the ones close by
To get the flavor of their existence
And why there were created, evolved
The very reason for their being
Their natural amenities; God's influence
Their man-made wonders; tall buildings
The different shops, neighborhoods, peoples
With their ethnic, cultural; other differences
That were reflected in these cities
When I was just a child
Wondering about cities

Evolution of a City

Take one river made by God
Add one roadway made by man
Sprinkle with a few homes for families
Add a few farms for food
Maybe a general store for goods
You're still in the country

Add a bridge to cross the river
Now you have a crossroads
An important point on the river
Gasoline station, stores, café a must
A motel, restaurant, more to follow
The urban scene is evolving

More hosing gathers all around
Young families; children, babies to follow
Creating the need for schools and daycare
Add public parks and open spaces
Police, fire, public works are now required
Other municipal functions evolve

Now you have a city, a community
The process takes varying lengths of time
Typically, a generation, a family phase
This is the evolutional cycle of a city
The development of a municipal government
That serves the needs of its people

Viewing America

Located next to natural amenities of great beauty
Waterways like beaches, bays, rivers, lakes
Unique geologic settings like mountains, canyons, coastlines
Full of man-made wonders for all to see
Crossroads, transportation systems, bridges
The architecture reflected in the buildings
This is how great cities evolved over the years

These natural and man-made wonders
In which people and their buildings evolved
And society and architecture developed
Existing side-by-side in the city
Reflections of our civilization
Our windows to the world
Allowing others to see us through our cities

Viewing America at its best, through these cities
With their seats of government; halls of governance
These showplaces for commerce, industry, technology
The centers of our arts and entertainment
And renowned educational institutions
Great achievements to man; society
Reflecting the accomplishments of our civilization

Cultural Windows

When cities were small, simple
They were the same in many ways
Their founders, their citizens, their new arrivals
Cultural homogeneity prevailed
And was commonplace
When cities were small
In America

The industrial revolution changed much
New industries, new products, new jobs
Rural, suburban; came in droves
Emigrants followed, en masse
These urban newcomers flourished
As well as their traditions and customs
From their regions and homelands

Now, heterogeneity in our cities prevails
Neighborhoods changed; permanently, new ways
Due to the influence of Hispanics, African-Americans
Italians, Greeks, Chinese. Koreans, South Americans too
The emigration of peoples continues, unabated
From other lands, many political refugees
Coming to the cities of America

With their unique cultures, traditions, and foods
Cities, our windows on the world; these lands
Other far away societies and cultures
That have transformed our cities
Windows on the world, without leaving home
Without leaving your city, community
Only in America, the international melting pot

In Retrospect

When life, livelihoods, were simple
Farmers provided the bounty of nature
Ranchers provided the wildlife
Fishermen provided the fruits of the sea
When life and jobs were simple
With wages low, jobs not many
In our villages, towns, and boroughs
This is how it was throughout the years

Meanwhile in our evolving cities
Merchants provided the commerce
Industrialists provided the industry
Other countries provided emigrants, refugees
Commerce and industry expanded
Fueled by the technologies of the time
Jobs and higher incomes for all
The lure of the city prevailed

People moved to the city, en masse
Including farmers, ranchers, fishermen
As well as emigrants and refugees
Population densities, land values, soared
Jobs everywhere; for everyone, anyone
Commerce and industry flourished
Technology, production, prevailed
Creating the exodus from country to city

Now people move to the suburbs
With second homes in the country
Vacation places in the hinterlands
Just to get away from the city
They buy their homes, raise their families
Away from the diversity and complexity
Of the industry and commerce
And the different peoples in the city

Awakening of a City

Today, for the first time in my life
I witnessed the awakening of a city
From the darkness of the night
To the dawn of a new day
From peaceful serenity, to flurried activity
From the loading unloading of goods
To the hustle of people buying them
These movements of the whole city

Five bells by the church!
First the birds singing before daybreak
Followed by the crack-of-dawn's light
Sidewalks, walkways, streets empty
The architecture of the buildings in view
The public infrastructure awaiting its purpose
The beginnings of urban life taking place
On this new day in the city

Six bells by the church!
The first lights in houses, people going to work
Then the delivery of goods to stock the stores
By trucks of six-, ten-, eighteen-wheels and more
Newspapers dropped off in bundles
Bakers baking at bakeries
Cooks in diners readying for their morning fare
Waitresses waiting to wait on their customers

Seven bells by the church!
Later in the morning, the sun shining
Automobiles emerging, soon to be traffic
The streets used, the parking lots fill
And people walking to work
Important people in suits with briefcases
Later shoppers surface to make crowds
The tempo of the city unfolds before my very eyes

This morning I witnessed a city come to life
The transportation of goods
The stocking the markets, stores, cafes

Along with the movement of people
Filling the offices and stores; the entire downtown
The use of the public infrastructure unfolds
Just another busy day in the city
The one I experienced today, for the first time

City Limits

The city is the land within the limits
The public structures; the parks, open spaces
The network of systems that hold it together
The architecture, the cityscape
Places to work and play
And shop
To live

The life of the city is its people
With their different ethnicities, cultures, traditions
Where they live, how they live
Together they live
In the city
To make it one
Whole

People live on the land within the limits
Put public structure, parks, open spaces, to work
Use the network of systems that make life possible
Make use of the architecture that creates the cityscape
They work, they live, they play
Those people in the city
Who are the city

Government, Governance

Government
The framework of a political institution
The exercise of authority over citizens
Through offices, departments, bureaus, divisions
Based on fundamental rules and principles
Written, codified; organized by function for all to see
Set by elected officials, representing the people
Administered by bureaucrats, government employees
Who run government on a daily basis
Treating all citizens equally; unequivocally
As they regulate the affairs of the community
With oversight through hearings, appeals
To their elected representatives
This is the process of government

Governances
The democratic process, a political process
Taking into consideration different views from all
Citizens, specials interest groups, lobbyists, others
Used when adopting fundamental rules and principles
To regulate the affairs of the community
With agendas, meetings; public hearings, debates
All matters settled through motions, voting
By duly elected representatives of the people
This is the process of governance, the democratic way
To be followed by bureaucrats, government employees
As they administer the affairs of a community
Set by the peoples' representatives
This is the process of governance

Do not confuse government with governance
Do not confuse governance with government
For government has to do with implementation
And governance has to do with legislation
Both separate stages of the democratic process
Those of adopting and administering
Those fundament laws and principles

Adopted by representatives who are elected
And administered by bureaucrats who are appointed
Both have their respective roles
In the process of government; governance
In the city; all cities

The Name Game

Why are cities called by so many confusing names?
In some states the name is nothing but a game!
Such as townships, towns, boroughs, villages
All these names, maybe more, just for cities
Too many names to remember, easy to forget
Maybe names I haven't even heard of yet

The original reason behind these names is simple
They relate to several legal species of cities
And to quite obscure aspects of English law
A town used to be a generic name for cities and boroughs
In New England a township is a portion of a county
And a town is a name for a village, borough, small city

Legally a town is a political subdivision of a state
Included in a county, which are sometimes called parishes
Having corporate powers of a municipality
A generic term used for incorporated cities of all types
Possessing those sacred powers of local self-government
Granted by the State in which they are contained

These terms could be arranged by a community's size
From city, to township, to borough, to town, to village
But as federal and state grants favored cities over the years
Local politicians lobbied to change their name
Merely to qualify for these grant funds
This is the reason these terms no longer make sense

Who Does What?

People think services come from city hall
Service delivery systems are mixed, diffused
Many services are not from city hall at all
But are delivered by a myriad of special districts
Agencies performing local community services
Like slices of a pie, layers of a cake
Small boxes in a public service matrix
This is how services are really provided

Sometimes called the "hidden layer" of government
These special districts, providing specific services
With boards appointed by other public officials
Overseen by overseers not elected to serve
These agencies with a life form of their own
Financed with public revenues from their services
Away from city hall, the scrutiny of the public
Yet their services are many, impact profound

The fastest growth area of local government
Providing services people take for granted
Away from the public's awareness, press too
Such as special sewer and water agencies
And cemetery, hospital, and park districts
Those for air and water quality, transit, too
Don't forget planning, lighting, many more
Just to name a few, of these special districts

The list is almost endless, depending upon the city
More in urban areas; fewer in the suburbs, country areas
Important services, yet hidden from public view
Taken for granted, yet paid by citizens, user fees
Led by non-elected leaders with public anonymity
Financed by user fees, other government's dues
Citizens should be concerned, about these agencies
These services not provided by their city hall

Very Special Districts

Government by special districts
The fastest growing layer of government
The one most hidden from the people
Sometimes without elected officials

With members appointed by other elected officials
Sometimes lay people appointed by councils
From cities; sometimes by formula, contract
These stewards of our tax dollars Unknown to the public
These specials districts
Overlapping our city boundaries
Providing services to citizens; unaware
Of their virtual existence

Their types too numerous to mention
The services they provide are many
Transit, planning, water, sewer, hospitals, and more
Many more, like cemeteries, street lighting, hospitals
Even vector control districts, tourist districts
To name a few, a very few, of these special districts
Whose operations are paid with local taxes
By people like you and I, average folks
With public meetings, unattended by the public
With budgets approved, unknown by citizens
Who pay for their keep
Through their taxes

These special districts
The hidden layers of government
The fastest growing government entities
Impacting us all, every day, in many ways
Without much public accountability, sometimes none
Operating in the shadow of the public sector
Without public awareness, scrutiny
That all public agencies deserve
These many special districts
Operating in your city, every day
Without your knowledge, but you pay
Through user fees or property taxes

The Public Infrastructure

Citizens take it for granted
Unless it is broken, dysfunctional
The public infrastructure
Those networks that comprise the city
These systems that make the city livable
That wear away with no replacement funds
That are repaired, replaced only when they break

There's the stuff above the ground
And the stuff below the ground
Connected with the stuff on the ground
Forming complex systems and networks
The larger the city the greater the complexity
Of these pieces of the municipal physical plant
That *comprise* the public infrastructure

It provides the essence of urban life
Like utilities and transportation systems
All the municipal public buildings and grounds
And don't forget parks and playgrounds
The sewer and water treatment plants a must
When these things work no one seems to care
A crisis must occur before they become an issue

These components of the public infrastructure
Those part of government people take for granted
Unless their components are broken, dysfunctional
To replacement funds here, higher priorities
Like financing public safety; police and fire
Typically, only funded when required
And citizens and politicians are forced to care

Civics Class

Most high school civics classes
That made us study the rights and duties of citizens
Although they lasted for an entire semester
Seem to start with the federal government
Then went on to cover the state government
And sometimes maybe counties too
But soon the semester ended

Without ever having examined cities
Those places where we all live and work
Spend most of our lives, pay property taxes
The places we should know most about
But don't ever learn
How quick the semester ended
In those civics classes

LESSON TWO

POLITICS AND POLITICIANS

Don't Forget to Vote!

Sometimes the best candidates get elected
And frequently they don't for many reasons
Sometimes the worst candidates get elected
And frequently they don't for many reasons
The deciding factors are many, some make no sense
During political campaigns, at election time

Such as the most political signs, or the largest
The smoothest speaker under fire, the fast talker
The largest ego, the most dominant personality
Those with the best soundbites on the air
Or others with large ads, or the most money
The list could go on and on, for endless reasons

Sometimes the people vote for the right reasons
And the best candidates get elected
Sometimes the people vote for the wrong reasons
And the best candidates don't get elected
The voters must take the time to be astute
To get to know the people behind the candidates

Our Elections

Elections use to be simple
When citizens lived in cities
And voted for their leaders
Who represented all of the people
Equally
This was true
Back when politics was simple

The representation of groups; happenstance
Not by design, law, or mandate
As cities grew, become more complex
Gerrymandering maintained the status quo
Political power bases remained in tact
Disenfranchisement began to take place
Slowly at first, then not so

Before to long, remedies were needed
Adjustments to the election process were many
District and at-large elections; combinations thereof
Alternative, limited, cumulative voting
Proportional representation too
To name a few; new election processes
For the time being

Surely new models will emerge
If not undertaken voluntarily; involuntarily
By law or mandate
To ensure the proper representation
Of the people in the city
All of the people in the city
Every city

The best election system is one
Voted upon by the people
Not required by state law
Nor by court mandate
The people should decide
If their elected leaders let them
Until then, surely more models will follow

Tickets Anyone!

The circus is not in town
No major show, or popular concert event
Not for Little League fund raisers
Nor for the Boy Scouts or Girl Scouts
Not even the Cub Scouts or Brownies
Or for a noble cause, in which to believe
But for politicians, attempting to raise funds
To beef-up their treasury's coffers
In an effort to finance their campaigns
Selling their tickets, at election time

Hitting-up unions, who need their support
And management folks, employees, contractors too
Those who feel beholden to the politicians
To their duly elected public officials
Those elected by the people, holding their trust
To determine the fate of their city, do its business
The politicians who vote upon the outcome
Of salary raise, fringe benefits, contracts, for all
These are the people asked to buy these tickets
By the politicians, one and all, at election time

25, 50, 100 bucks a pop, that's the price
For those tickets, these fund-raising events
As they are frequently, euphemistically, called
A lot of money for the average folks
Impacting the pockets, these employees and contractors
With families to support, savings to garner
Who feel beholden, obligated, to buy these tickets
From the ticket vendors, their elected officials
Who expect a show of loyalty, at election time
By buying these tickets, for these political events

Unethical, amoral, without justification
In fact, should be against the law
Selling these tickets, to those beholden
Sales are sometimes brisk, nonetheless
From contractors doing work for the city

Those unions seeking favors, future votes
And those management folks, seeking recognition
From other employees, for whatever the reason
Who want to be recognized, given their due
By these city politicians, after election time

Good Political Donations

Generally, a good thing, the democratic way!
Small donations from many people
As well as the business community
To get their favorite candidate elected
The one with the agenda with support
Who can solve their problems
Or agrees with their particular specials interest
Maybe a promise to hold-down taxes
A few of the wealthy and astute
Give to all of the candidates
And they have access to the victors
No matter who wins
Regardless of their agenda, party affiliation
At election time
In the city

Bad Political Donations

Sometimes a bad thing!
Those large donations from business persons
And the members of the corporate community
Generally, to the political incumbents
Who vote to use their services
To do business with the community
The bankers, lawyers, the bond counsels
The financial institutions, law firms, consultants
As contractors, vendors, suppliers of all types
Who want to continue providing
Their goods and services to the city
As they have in the past
Question their donations, contributions
At election time
In the city

Circling the Wagons

The mayor, council, together the governing body, important folks
Elected by the voters to serve as legislators, the overseers
These holders of the ultimate public trust, by election of the people
Of their municipal corporation, the city, their community
One of their most important duties, that of hiring the chief executive
Title varies depending upon city charters, state laws, regional differences
City manager, city administrator, chief administrative officer, to name a few

Almost without exception, hired by majority vote
To serve at the pleasure, sometimes whim, of elected officials
Hired to manage the city; its daily operations, sole responsibility
Oversees all departments; hirings, firings, promotions too
Works with all department managers, circling the wagons
To do what the elected leaders desire, by majority vote, continually
Onward to the future, new goals, new horizons, services, programs

That change from election to election, almost without exception
Which redefines the future, new goals, new horizons; again
Always, from campaign to campaign, every few years
This is the role of elected officials: philosophical direction
And the role of the chief executive: administrative responsiveness
For the municipal organization; departments, employees one and all
In the typical city, in nearly all communities, in America

Politics v. Political Leadership

Politics
I've seen it many times
Elected leaders seeking the path of least resistance
Voting for what is most politically expedient
Voting for what is popular
Voting to please the crowd
Voting to satisfy a special interest
This is politics

Political leadership
Elected leaders making difficult decisions
Voting with the publics' interest in mind
Voting for the good-of-the-whole
Voting to settle unpopular issues
Voting against a specials interest
Voting with the future in mind
This is political leadership

Mayors: The Good Ones

Elected by the people to serve the public
To be the city's chief elected official
The chairman of their governing body
The interface between the city and its government
And the ceremonial leader of the community
The good mayors know their roles and duties
Fulfilling them with grace and dignity

They generate citizen interest in major issues
And solidify public sentiments for important programs
Act as chief lobbyist for the city's political agenda
Serving as legislative and advocate for the city
With higher levels of government
They garner citizen support for needed legislation
They gather the votes and dollars to implement

They ride the municipal bureaucracy
To make it responsive to the community
And serve as the focal point for citizen complaints
Helping to resolve unresolved problems and issues
At the lowest levels of city government
In many city halls in our cities
Throughout America

Mayors: The Bad Ones

Elected by the people to serve the public
To be the city's chief elected official
The chairman of their governing body
The interface between the city and its government
And the ceremonial leader of the community
The good mayors know their roles and duties
The bad ones don't and problems arise

They try to steal the spotlight and attention
From the other members of the governing body
By trying to resolve problems and issues in a vacuum
Taking all the credit unless their efforts go awry
Always trying to be center stage in the municipal show
Not working with their elected colleagues
Making a mockery of the democratic process

They call whoever will listen to solve a problem
Frequently at the lowest levels of the bureaucracy
And with problems and issues of an insignificant nature
Without following the chain-of-command
They follow none because they are the mayor
In many city halls in our cities
Throughout America

Spoils v. Merit

Sometimes mayors seek competency
Although loyalty may be more important
When filling key positions
In a mayor's administration
To advance his/her political agenda
To the victor goes the spoils!
This is the way it is supposed to be
In the strong mayor form of government

Professional managers always want competency
And personal loyalty doesn't even play a part
When filling key positions
In a city's administration
Merit is involved
To hire the best candidate to serve the public
This is the way it is supposed to be
In the council-manager form of government

As a taxpayer, which do you prefer?
The spoils or the merit hiring system?
Personal loyalty or professional competency
As a taxpayer, the answer should be quite clear
Common sense should be the judge
Just like hiring people in the private sector
At least this is the way you think it should be
Depending upon the form of government

The Best and the Brightest?

In the private sector
The corporate world
The best and the brightest are always hired
Those with the best experience and credentials
The highest achievers, the best performers
To run America's the best performers
To run America's corporations
Almost without exception
Making America leader in the world
Providing goods and services
At the most reasonable cost
An admirable goal to seek!

In the public sector
The municipal world
Sometimes folks are hired
Those with political connections
And known by the governing body
The community
Its board of directors
Limiting the gene pool of qualified candidates
And the ability to get the best and the brightest
Not in the best interests of citizens
The major stockholders of the corporation
Of our City Halls, throughout America!

The Union Gamble

Traditionally a good thing
Negotiating for better wages, benefits
And improved working conditions
For the members of their bargaining unit
Through labor contracts
Negotiated with management
And approved by elected officials
Required by law throughout the nation

Sometimes not a good thing
When wages, benefits are good
And working conditions are fine
And the cost-of-living is down
Increased salaries, fringes unlikely
Unless the union backed candidates
With hard and or soft-dollars
During the last political campaign

If the union candidates win
It's pay-off time for the employees
Larger salary increases, more fringes
If the union candidates lose
It's pay-back time for their employees
By the successful elected officials
Smaller increases, less fringes, possible layoffs
It's a gamble the union should not take

Political Preferences

It's almost always the case
With few exceptions
What gets funded, what doesn't
Is it what the public wants?
Or a mere political preference!

When the politicians fund programs
It's always the same three
Police, fire, and public works
The highest profile services
With the largest employee unions

When the politicians don't fund programs
It's always the same three
Libraries, recreation, and human services
Is it the desire of the public?
Or the size of the labor unions!

Decisions in the best interest of the public?
Or what generates the most votes!
I've seen it many times
It never changes, probably never will
These votes at budget time

Those Public Meetings

A good thing for government
And for public officials
When citizens speak-out, sound-off
Stating their views on those issues
That influence their lives
And their neighborhoods
As well as their city
In public meetings
At city hall

It helps open-minded politicians
More objectively make up their minds
When deciding upon important issues
Facing their community
This is the goal, the purpose
Of the sacred democratic process
That of soliciting public input
In public meetings
At city hall

This process becomes dysfunctional, goes awry
When only the dooms-dayers and nay-sayers attend
Those against a project, program, plan, or policy
Who show up to speak at public meetings
And their citizens and taxpayers don't
Because they are too busy with other commitments
To become involved in the democratic process
In public meetings
At city hall

LESSON THREE

THE URBAN SCENE

The Differences: Where Have They Gone?

The experience of travel use to be great
From city to city, throughout America
The differences were everywhere
In tastes, dress, preferences, foodstuffs
In our neighborhoods, on the streets
And life in general, in our cities
Each one was unique onto itself

Many differences began to disappear
Slowly at first, then not so over time
Now the sameness of cities prevails
Exceeding their unique characteristics
No need to ask why, progress is the reason
Our cities are the same
Regardless of their location

Progress that has created, facilitated
National brands, chain stores, franchises
For markets, restaurants, businesses
Insuring uniformity of goods and services
Creating conformity among the people
Whose tastes, preferences are now determined
By these outside sources; market forces

Where have the differences gone?
Of the people living in our cities
Progress is the answer
These differences are dwindling away
The differences that will never return
Market forces prevail; people acquiesced
Creating cities of sameness and banality

Old Urbanism, New Urbanism?

Urbanism and urbanists, city planning by another name
These folks concerned with the design of our cities
The new urbanists, those neo-traditionalists
Who favor going back in time, history; to a safe place
Erecting new cities, like the ones of olden days gone by
Full of new Georgian, Victorian, and Colonial homes
These old-looking new houses with their porches, fences, back yards
Laid out with narrow streets; mixed land uses, jobs close by

With town centers and village greens, like it used to be
As if something was wrong with modernism; current trends
Progressive thoughts, or regressive nostalgia?
Trying to bring about social change through architecture
By the way our cities are designed, or should be
Against the modern trends, the avant-guard, the nuevo
Being built for the proletariat, not the bourgeois, they say
Yet who ultimately can afford to pay the price will decide

As the railroads undermined the automobile
So did freeways and highways destroy our cities
Built by government and their officials: federal, state, and local
They created the public infrastructure for the suburbs
Based on political criteria, not architectural ones
These were government decisions made by politicians
Not architects using principles of sound urban design
These new urbanists, neo-traditionalist, of the new urbanism

Trying to create cities as if they had no automobiles
These rich developments, built on the edges of towns
Sprawl under another name, new suburbs, suburbia?
Maybe not new towns, but the next best thing
To living in a real city, yet in the suburbs
Nothing like the real thing, America's older cities
A grass-roots planning movement, or building utopias?
Let the public, not the planners, decide!

Traditional Urban Design

America's older cities were designed
With town centers and village greens in mind
Surrounded by city halls and churches
With centers of commerce to scale
And small shops close by to serve all
Ringed by residential areas
The schools not far away
And certainly, no mall
Or large discount stores
This is the way cities were
Without urban sprawl
In a time gone by

Contemporary Urban Design

New cities were not designed
They evolved; virtually sprung up
Along major streets and highways
Sometimes mass-transit corridors
There urban landscape is always the same
Convenience stores, fast-food places; all franchises
And large discount stores of all types
With new residential developments not far away
Catering to the middle-class commuter; family
Designed to fit their pocketbook; lifestyle
The center of their community life is the mall
They define urban sprawl; are urban sprawl
They were really not designed at all
These new cities

Planned Growth?

Every city has a planning department
And miles of unsightly urban sprawl
Did they design it that way?
Those city planners in our cities
Responsible for their growth
But winding up with urban sprawl!

Those places along major streets
Leading from cities, to cities, between cities
Housing businesses to fix our homes, feed our faces
Repair and fuel our automobiles
And little more; that urban sprawl
That connects our cities

In all places and spaces
In America's cities
With planning departments
And city planners
Doing city planning
For the future of our cities

Buildings and People

The buildings are the structures
Those improvements upon the land
Made by man for mankind; society
That provide the architecture
In which our institutions are housed
That create the physical appearance
And the skyline, of our cities

These buildings seem to stay
Seems like forever, throughout the years
While the uses in them change over time
And the people in them come and go
From generation to generation
This cycle continues unabated
Almost without exception

Commercial uses change over time
From general stores, to specialty shops, to boutiques
To vacant buildings in some parts of town
Many wee monuments to the corporate world
Some were legacies of community pillars
As fortunes change so does commerce
Old buildings decay, new ones take their place

Residential uses do the same
From single family, to multiple-family, to tenement houses
Passing from the middle-class to those less fortunate
Being occupied by different emigrant groups
That seem to come and go throughout the years
Moving in and moving out, some moving up
As the buildings change, so do the people

Buildings become the architecture
Their uses and the people occupying them
Seem to change with the passage of time
From new, to old, to decay, to worse
In some parts of town, many parts of town
Facilitated by the middle-class flight
From our cities to the suburbs

Private Public Places

We all want more public places in our cities
Citizens demand it, society expects it
Government is pressured to acquire it
These public places in our cities
Typically build at the taxpayers' expense
For all to enjoy, from now to eternity
Present and future generations alike

But wait!
Can public places be private?
Can government grant greater height limits?
Allow higher land-use densities?
Permit smaller setback requirements?
Grant economic tradeoffs for the public good
All in exchange for more public places

More public places for citizens to enjoy
Such as streetscapes and landscaped areas
And walk-throughs and walkways
Even atriums and mini-parks
All on private property, private expense
With unrestricted public access
For all citizens to enjoy, forever

All in exchange for deviations to
Standard building and zoning regulations
These standards that are uniformly imposed
With rare exception to the rule
Without the goal of more public places in mind
Hence development occurs
Approved by the governments of our cities

The private sector can pay for public places
These private public places may fill the need
The need to close the gap between
Citizen expectations and the public spaces
And the desire for more public places
Built with private money for the public to enjoy
And to make our cities more livable for all

Evolution of the Foot-Path

First there was the foot-path, then the trail
Usually the shortest distance between two places
The trail followed the well-traveled path
That evolved into the dirt roadway
Later turning into the paved residential street
Which becomes the major arterial street

Development continues, urbanization unfolds
From the arterial street to the commercial corridor
Then a parkway, a highway, finally a freeway
The evolutionary cycle is always the same
The trail that people walked in the country
Later becomes the freeway they drive to the city

This cycle fueled by cars, driven by people
All designed to move people in cars
From neighborhood to neighborhood, city to city
And goods from the manufacturer
To our commercial centers: cities and malls
And finally, to serve as a venue for traffic jams

Once the cycle evolves, is complete
The freeway will never be a highway
The highway never to be a parkway
The parkway never to be a major arterial
The major arterial, a residential street no more
Only history shows foot-paths and trails

People now take weekend trips
To walk on foot-path and trails
To avoid traffic and congestion
Along freeways and highways
And so, this cycle continues
To accommodate our progress?

Freeway and Highways

Freeways and highways
Signs of contemporary urban life
Models of efficient mass transportation
The ideal vehicle for the automobile
Moves myriad people to their destinations
Using multiples of one-way lanes
Via vast urban asphalt corridors
Surrounded by sprawl; empty places
With thousands of unknown faces
Along the way
Freeways and highways

Driving Forces

Sometimes I think the automobile
Has had more of a dramatic impact
In the planning of our cities
Than city planners have had
Even though automobiles
Are not trained in the science
Of city planning

After all is considered
And after all is said and done
Planners only set forth land uses
Through master plans and zoning laws
And their subdivision regulations
That create the future design
Of our cities, they think?

Automobiles on the other hand
Dictate the number of our streets
Their design, where they're located
Along with traffic islands and signals
Public and private parking lots
Those places to house and store them
While we work, shop, and sleep

Who has the greater impact?
On the design of our cities
Planners or automobiles!
While planners drive automobiles
Automobiles also drive planners
And the design of the urban environment
In our cities

People Drive Cars, Cars Drive Sprawl

People drive their cars in cities
Cars drive cities and their people
They drive more than people
They drive the sprawl
That ugly urban sprawl
That dominates, permeates
Each of our cities, everyone
Those car lots, both new and used
Those gasoline and lubrication stations
Those maintenance and repair shops
Those paint and parts joints
Those tire and transmission stores
Those muffler and brake places
Those quickly tune-up centers

And don't forget!
Those numerous drive-through lanes
Evolving all over in our cities
And the need for those freeways
With their diamond express lanes
And the miles of parking lots
With their millions of parking spaces

Most of our urban sprawl
Seems to be related to our mode of transportation
That singularly important man-made invention
That we all have, the multi-passenger automobile
Almost always with one driver per car
That we all drive – everywhere, every day
In our cities full of urban sprawl

Cities Without Malls

Nice to see a city without a mall!
That has sucked the life from its downtown
Where the Main Street is still vibrant and alive
With stores, cafes, restaurants, movie theatres
And most all families walking, children playing
People of all types, walks of life
Walking on Main Street
Their Main Street
In their city

On, these cities without malls, what a sight!
What an old-fashioned experience!
What a slice of urban life; of society
What are increasingly few and far between
These Main Streets, our Main Streets
Focal points of community
The commercial centers of our cities
That are fastly disappearing
From America's urban landscape

Feeding our Faces

We all go to those places
That provide food to feed our faces
In most all places, urban spaces
That dot the landscape
Of our cities
One-and-all

The fast-food franchises
Those national chain restaurants
Delicatessens, diners, cafes too
And those fancier places
They all feed our faces
In congested urban places

As incomes increase over time
The number of these places
Permeates all urban spaces
With a total disregard
To the urban design
Of our cities

Advertising Everywhere!

Seems like many places and spaces
Especially public places and open spaces
Are full of advertising, announcements
Of all types, forms, shapes, and sizes
Selling goods and services, relentlessly
For individuals of all incomes and tastes
To people who do not want them

Billboards, signs, handbills, sandwich boards
Freestanding, attached; horizontal, vertical
In your mail, in your face, everywhere
Frequently illuminated with bright lights
Trying to catch our attention in the night
As the markets change so does the message
That lures us to buy these goods and services

In the future look for more of the same
Our public places and open spaces adorned
And plastered with advertising of all forms
It's the American way, the free-market right
Until every space and place is filled
With more of these unwanted unsightly messages
Advertising, advertising; there is no end in sight

Nature's Best: Our Coastlines

Those special and unique places
That were created by God
The best that nature has to offer
These peaceful coastlines of beauty
That define the geographic limits
Of our continents, nations, states, and cities

These resting places for oceans
Sometimes expanding their influence
Over lost ground, redefining places
We all go to watch; view with awe
Wishing we could experience them forever
These wondrous natural coastlines

Although a part of nature
Some coastlines are private property
Even though, man should not be allowed
To change or modify them in any way
They should be held in trust; perpetuity
For all future generations to enjoy

These one-of-a-kind coastlines
Created by God for all to enjoy
Not for anyone to change for his needs
But for man to adapt to nature
A natural beauty, not to be altered
Except by nature over the centuries

Another Tree

What a beautiful tree
Been around for a century, at least
With its large trunk, deep roots
And hundreds of branches, leaves
Providing shade, works of art
That capture the snow, deflect the rain
These natural wonders
For all to enjoy

One-hundred years to grow, maybe more
Only a moment to cut down, remove
For no reason, for any reason, with ease
With that man-made wonder, the chain saw
How quickly they're made to disappear
Never to be seen again, these trees
A part of our neighborhoods, streets, lives
I wish they could defend themselves!

LESSON FOUR

THE GOVERNMENT

Our City Halls

City Hall is a building
It is not government
It does not represent the public
It does not set public policy
It does not manage
It does not provide services
It is but a mere structure

Government is a process
Many people make it happen
Elected leaders, top management
As well as department managers
The dynamic interchange of all
Gives City Hall its life
And makes government work

And don't forget the citizens
Major stakeholders of this corporation
Who elect their leaders
And hold them accountable, responsive
For their community, public policies
Who provide continual feedback to all
About the job they are doing

City Hall is not government
It is but merely a building
Where government takes place
The interaction of public officials
Both elected and appointed
And the citizens who foot-the-bill
They make government a reality

The Legislative Body

Every city has one, a mayor
All cities have a city council, name and numbers vary
Typically depending upon the size of the community
Together they make up the governing board, body politic
These selected leaders, elected by citizens, serving the public
To provide municipal leadership; policies, direction
By majority vote, 51 percent; designed to please all
For the city's chief executive, department managers too
Through their votes, services and programs approved
It's their elective duty, responsibility
Primarily the same in all communities

The mayor, chairman of the board
The city's highest elected official, the focal point
And the chief elective officer, ceremonial head too
The leader of the community, power of the bully pulpit
Chairperson of the governing body, its meetings
Trying to push his/her agenda: services, programs
To lead the community in the future, right direction
The mayor's vision of what should be, could be
A powerful position, not your humble public servant
Sometimes with the right to vote, sometimes not
This is the role of mayors

The city council, board of directors
Those folks who decide upon matters, one and all
Who approve services, programs, staffing
The adopters of the annual budget; fees, charges
Which approves all municipal expenses, revenues
And capital projects too, improvements, real property
Owned by the community, municipal corporation
The ominous setters of tax rates, every one
The role of the city council; decisive, important
Of which the mayor, voting rights, is a member
These are the duties of the body politic

Elected Officials, Public Managers

Those mayors and city council members
Elected by the people, to serve the citizens
The ultimate holders of the people's trust
Of which municipal managers are not
Since they are merely hired to perform
To work for those elected representatives
This is how it will always be, should be
The role of those elected versus managers

The elected officials report directly to the people
Each tests their popularity at election time
They are there for a term, sometimes more
While municipal managers' report to the body politic
They make recommendations, advisory in nature
And implement the policies of elected leaders
Notwithstanding how they are bastardized
During the democratic process by majority vote

Personal differences, philosophies aside
Municipal managers merely implement, carry-out
This is their role, they should never forget
Their power is not with the people
They are there to please the elected officials
Impartially, objectively, unequivocally, always
Regardless if they think their smarter, know more
Than the holders of the ultimate trust of the people

The Legal Advisor

The chief legal advisor of the city
Called city attorney; West Coast
Goes by the name of corporation counsel; East Coast
Regardless of the name, does the same thing
Top legal advisor to the governing body
The legislators of the city; mayor, city council
Provides legal assistance to boards and commissions
And the chief executive officer, department managers too
Checks-out contracts, other municipal agreements
Gives the "nod" of approval before they are signed
Tries to reduce the city's liability exposure
Fewer lawsuits; counters the litigiousness of society
Not much contact with the general public
No need to be; regardless of the title, community
A staff job; little interface with the general public
The city attorney, corporation counsel
The legal expert of the municipality
In every city
In America

The City Clerk

The city clerk, every city has one
Keeper of the official documents, records
Those pieces of paper important to people
Birth, death certificate; marriage licenses
Documents important to the owners of stuff
Like land deeds, financial instruments, titles
For official papers important to citizens
Notices, agendas, minutes; legal documents
The actions of their elected officials
Going back in time; time immemorial
To the first year of incorporation
These things important for posterity
The records of the city, for its people
To document the city's history
For all to see; present, future generations
The official archivist of the community
The ultimate holder of the public trust
The city clerk
In your city
In America's cities

The Buck Passes Through

Funds come in, funds go out – all fiscal year long
Citizens call it money, their cash, taxes
Finance folks call it funds, revenues, public coffers
Two categories of funds; discretionary, restricted
Discretionary revenues from local sources; taxes fees
Restricted revenues from other sources; grants, bequeaths
The former may be spent on anything, the latter earmarked
These two funds comprise the annual budget
Total budget minus restricted funds = local tax effort
Funds in/out, managed in between, ultimate accountability
To the public for discretionary funds
To other sources for restricted funds
All revenues in coffers; accounted by funding source, amount

The tasks of a city's finance director; varied, many
Treasurer over revenues due; the master collector, revenue manager
Investment of idle public funds, optimal returns, safety; the investor
Comptroller of all payments; the pay master, check signer
Oversees the acquisition of goods and services; the purchaser
In charge of raising debt, paying debt; the debt manager
In many cities responsible for tax assessments, tax collections too
Vital role in the budget process, this arduous annual task
Right-hand of the municipal chief executive, financial stuff
Important staff function, serving all departments equally
Responsible for the annual audit, sometimes by contract
Reconciles annual budget with expenses; by fund, department
Provided accountability to elected officials, citizens

Vital role played by elected officials, municipal finance
Approvers of the annual budget, authorized positions, expenses
Official setters of tax rates, under watchful eyes of citizens
Adopters of local user charges and fees, for services rendered
Finance director prepares, chief executive recommends
The budget, user charges and fees, municipal tax rates
Chief executive held accountable; finance director delegated

These various components of the annual financial cycle
These financial tasks, those responsible, held accountable
Ultimately to elected leaders, the electorate, all taxpayers
Those who elect the leaders pay the taxes they impose
To finance their public services, quality of life
In their community, every community

The Fire Service

Recently renovated a century-old fire station
Really not a lot of renovations to make
From horse-drawn wagons to machine-driven trucks
From a few hundred gallons of water to thousands
Had to widen the entrance bays
Since trucks are wider than wagons once were
Installed diesel fuel exhaust systems too
Because trucks use fuel and horses ate hay
Not much else had changed over the years

Except for the firemen's living conditions
With their microwave ovens and other appliances
And television sets with video cassette players
Don't forget the weight room to keep them in shape
And since hoses had replaced buckets
No longer need those tall towers to dry them
Since synthetic ones no longer need special care
The parking lot had to be expanded
Since more firemen now drive to work

One astute fire chief once commented
That the typical fire department reflects
Over a century of continuous public service
Unaffected by technological progress
But maybe the biggest change is
Over the decades and throughout the years
Is that of quicker and improved responses
Since trucks are faster than horse-drawn wagons
And hoses extinguish fires quicker than bucket brigades

Those Human Services

Those services with a question mark
Human services to citizens: the needy and poor
Those with negative predilections, afflictions
Citizens in need of help, personal problems
A human condition created by people
Each responsible for their own plight
The homeless and the hungry, some worse
In need of shelter and food, human needs
From cities who are coping with the basics
Of which these receive little attention
In most, nearly all, of our cities

Who should provide these human services?
Some say families, churches, social agencies
It's the American way, solving your own problems
Many cities provide some services, almost none
Depending upon the nature of their elected leaders
Liberal, conservative; fiscal constraints, heated debates
These services vary greatly from city to city
With no continuity between communities
After all, they are not a part of the basics
That citizens expect for their property taxes
Such as police, fire, and public works

Perhaps the federal and state governments
With their elected national and state leaders
Should provide leadership, provide these services
After all, these governments are better financed
From income taxes, tied to inflation
These national and state leaders should decide
And provide needed funds to needy cities
Who are grappling with the basics
And have little extra funds for these essentials
The hotly-debated human services ones
Needed to improve our human condition

The Library

Storing information; for centuries
To make literature available to the masses
Who would otherwise not be exposed
Because they could not afford them
And the old volumes; no longer available
These books; these "windows to the world"
The medium of storage has always been the written page
Until the world of microcomputers; their software
RAM's, CD-ROM's; megabytes, gigabits of storage
For new books, all types of information, everywhere
Are available through electronic terminals
Centrally stored, catalogued, accessible, retrievable
Stored on computer chips for instant access
By the masses, who now look at books
Books without pages, covers; formerly placed on shelves
In the future, accessible from home
These books, these "windows to the world"
Formerly the written word, now words on screens
For the world to see, on new electronic medium
Stored on computer chips, archived no longer
As they been in the past
For many centuries
At libraries

Evolving Park and Rec. Services

The fun part of the city, department status
Manages the parks, open spaces too
Determines recreational uses; public areas
Both active, sports; and passive, hiking trails
Public uses change with the times; publics' interest
From baseball, football, to soccer fields
Trying to limit public liability, exposure
Avoiding lawsuits from these public amenities
Draining wading ponds, fountains, swimming pools
Playgrounds from steel; to rubber, wood
Eliminating asphalt surfaces, to softer surfaces
Eliminating sand boxes, due to contamination
Serving the public, while limiting city's liability
Parks and recreation, vital components of the city
Resolving conflicts of service, liability exposure
These parks and recreation departments
Serving the city, the public caught in the middle
In all cities
Throughout the nation

Planners and Planning

Planners plan, that's their job in the city
In those planning departments, everywhere
With their general plans, land use guides, zoning laws
Subdivision regulations, codes, and the like
Important planning documents, one and all
Devised to design the community
To separate dissimilar land uses
Keeping homes away from industries
Industries away from commercial properties
In neatly packaged areas, from city to city

Planners plan better in new communities
Like the ones in the West, not in the East
Yet urban sprawl, traffic congestion result
Seems worse where planning should work best
Leads many planners to search for model communities
With town centers and village greens, as in the past
With mixed land uses, where citizens can live and work
That now exist in the older areas of the nation
Developed before planning became a profession
Before it evolved from an art form to a science

Those planners; doing their plans, planning
With their impressive legal documents
Trying to determine what's best for us
For the city, neighborhood, specific sites
Do they really make a difference?
Those planners, in those planning departments
Trying to improve the urban landscape
Like the cities of long ago, in a time gone by
In places not so far away
That were designed before there were planners

Police Patrols

In our police departments
The very essence of law enforcement
It started out by cops walking the beat
In their assigned neighborhoods
Everyone knew their cop, he knew them
He knew all – the good and the bad
On his assigned foot patrol
In his neighborhood, on his beat
It's the way it always was

Then, soothing new arrived on the scene
Assembly lines made automobiles less expensive
Police patrol vehicles were designed
With guns, cages, and restraints
Outfitted with radios, central dispatching
The ideal device, the perfect vehicle
To hunt down, capture, hold, the bad guys
With these police patrol cars
In their assigned sector within the city

All cities used them, modern stuff
These police patrols in special cars
Day-in and day-out, night after night
Responding to calls-for-service
Catching the bad guys
When someone makes a call
And they are dispatched to respond
Motor patrols in, foot patrols out
It was a sign of the times

Not all was right with these cops
Doing patrols in their police cars
Not knowing the people, any people
In the neighborhoods, on the street
Out of touch with the good guys
Losing tough with the bad guys
Who's in the patrol car
No one seemed to know

Except the police in dispatching
During the last decade all has changed
It's back to the future, police practices
Community policing, neighborhood patrols
Cops being assigned to walk the streets again
Getting to know the citizens they serve
Dealing with their families, children
As well as their local merchants
Following-up on their complaints
Solving their problems, on the beat

Just like they had done in the past
These cops walking the beat
The way it was before patrol cars
Cops knowing the names of citizens
People calling their cops by name
The way it used to be, should be
In our police departments
Where cops are hired to serve, protect
The citizens, merchants, they serve

Essential Public Works

Those services most folks take for granted
Unless they are broken, an annoyance, or unsafe
Those provided by public works departments
Our streets, sidewalks; transportation systems
Refuse collection, recycling; human wastes
Wastewater, stormwater, treatment services
And a city's public buildings and grounds
Including its playgrounds, parks, open spaces
The essence of the city, its public infrastructure
Primary components in its quality-of-life
People expect these services, demand them
For the payment of their property taxes
Regardless of their form of government
Level of wealth, or geographic location
In every city, all cities
Throughout America
Public works services

The Technology Battle

Cities and the use of new technologies
Difficult to implement; mindset of elected officials
Holding down cost, budgets, tax rates
Copiers, fax machines, computers, and the like
First, one per floor, probably like the telephone
Then one per office, then one for each workstation
How quickly they forget, those elected officials
That technology helps serve the public
Goal is copies, fax machines, computers
For each department, workstation, employee in the city
An uphill battle, worth fighting
To improve public services to citizens
Through the use of these new technologies
Selling them to elected officials; cost-effective, yet difficult
Regardless of the city, geographic location
The use of these modern technologies
To help make public employees more productive
In the city, all cities
Throughout the nation

The Ideal Model

Our finest private corporations
They all operate essentially the same
Their hierarchical structure that is
They have a chief executive officer
With a chairman of the board
And a board of directors
Satisfying their stockholders
Serving their customers
Making a profit
It's the American Way!

Our finest municipal corporations
They all operate essentially the same
Their hierarchical structure that is
They have a chief administrative officer
With a mayor
And a city council
Satisfying their electorate
Serving their citizens
Keeping taxes down
It's the American Way!

This model should be the same
Chief executive officer = chief administrative officer
Chairman of the board = mayor
Board of directors = city council
Stockholders = electorate
Customers = citizens
Profits = taxes
The people should expect no less
This corporate model
Of American Excellence!

LESSON FIVE

FROM THE TRENCHES

The Campaign Promise

Sometimes during a past election time
One mayoral candidate promised
He would provide jobs to city residents
A great campaign promise
That no one would disagree
City jobs for us, not them
A real vote getter!

When confronted that this was against the law
The mayoral candidate responded
This was a part of his platform
And if it was against the law
He would just blame me
For his inability to deliver
To implement this campaign promise

He was elected, became the mayor
Went to deliver on this lofty promise
Trying to get jobs for city residents
Was told it was against the law
And he was right, he just blamed me
For his inability to deliver
And citizens thought this was true

This was the new mayor
And one of his campaign promises
Which proved to be untrue
This other campaign promise came true
Since he did blame me
He was the good guy
I was the rue!

The Invocation

An important day, a ribbon cutting
For some particular event, service
Potentates, public invited; mayor to officiate
Starting with the obligatory invocation
Stated so right in the program
For this official public occasion
Should have been a routine rite
This brief, simple, invocation

The ministers were selected by rotation
This turn was a Buddhist Monk
From the only monastery in town
He was confirmed, all arrangement made
Until the mayor saw the program
And said never again, this Buddhist Monk
This Japanese-American, man of the cloth
Selected to give this invocation

How was one to know, that the mayor
A retired Army Sergeant, some 30-years
Of Philippine ancestry, served in World War II
Was a survivor of the Bataan Death March
In a battle against the Japanese, four decades ago
It proved that some memories don't fade
And that war leaves deep, lasting, wounds
Even with the passage of time

A Lesson in Politics

Was called to the mayor's office one day
Mayor asked the minister to raise his concern
About making repairs to the church parking lot
Then the mayor asked for my help
To use city work crews, this worthwhile project
After all it was a church, a house of worship
And that's why I was there
To make the mayor look good
In the eyes of the minister and his flock

Promptly told the minister that we would not help
Since the church was private property, not public
And it wasn't right to do at the taxpayers' expense
That was the way it always was; this line of distinction
The minister thanked the mayor for his assistance
The mayor thanked me for my help
I was the bad guy this day; many days
As the mayor and minister walked away
Mumbling my name in vain

Later that day, seeing the mayor, I said
"You knew we couldn't do that!"
"Public and private property and all"
"So why did you ask for my help!"
On this problem we could not resolve
It was a waste of time, one and all
More important things beckoned my call
And certainly, the minister; church and flock
To which the mayor responded

"When there's good news I will tell them"
"When its bad news I'll let you tell them"
This was the mayor's philosophy, operating style
And this became the day I learned the difference
Between mayors and managers
Politics and administration
And this rule has held true, remained constant
Throughout the years
To this very day

Seeking the Grant

A new and exciting state grant
For which we did not quality
File the announcement, case closed
This should be it, end of the story
The tale goes on, more to follow
Like the politics of the city

Mayor shouts "we must apply for this grant"
Even though we both knew, very well
That we did not meet the requirements
And our application would be rejected
End in a failure, known in advance
But wait, a politician must look good

The press coverage was great
"City Applies for Grant"
Mayor quoted throughout
Public accolades to the mayor
For trying to acquire a new program
Doing his job, seeking this grant

It is better to apply, and be rejected
Then never to have applied at all
It helps you look good to the citizens
Gives you something to talk about
This effort at creativity, innovation
Failure can always be blamed on others

Welcome to the world of politics
Of seeking positive press coverage
And the need to look good to the public
Where no news coverage really existed
But must be created, orchestrated with flare
By the mayor seeking the grant

The Ticket Fix

One day in the city, a typical day
The Mayor received a ticket
On his way to give a speech
Doing his civic duty, no doubt
Parking in the red, in a hurry
Gave it to the Chief of Police
To do the right thing; after all
He was the Mayor, giving a speech
The highest elected official
A municipal potentate, highest order
Acting like a typical scofflaw
On this typical day in the city

I know this story well!
Because the Chief called me immediately
And said "What should I do?"
With the Mayor's request to fix the ticket
I told the Chief, as a matter of fact
"Do what your conscience dictates"
"As you have in the past with other people"
Those who've wanted their tickets fixed
I never heard from the Chief again
Not even the Mayor, certain to tell
On a Chief that did not fix his ticket
Another typical day in the city

The Socialist

Quite a novelty in the local election
Any election, for that matter
A member of the Socialist Workers Party
Running for a seat on the city council
To represent those voters
Who later became his constituents
After he won the election

What impact could he have?
Sought council support for the international labor movement
And political backing for an underground gorilla war
Somewhere in South America, a world away
In a country that makes no difference
On the local political scene
Having failed, settled it, politically

Quite a nice guy
With a weird political agenda
When strange issues surfaced
That caught his unusual attention
International issues and local politics
The votes were never there, anywhere
On these issues of no import, that lacked support

Sometimes I wonder
With the fall of communism
Demonstrating the failure of socialism
What he is doing now; older, wiser?
A democrat, republican; liberal, conservative?
Or did he find a new cause
Something to set him apart from the fray!

In the local political arena
Dominated by taxes, potholes, stray dogs
And other issues of a non-partisan nature
No support for international causes, issues
No home for the Socialist Workers Party
Not in this local government
At city hall, in this city

Undercover Operation

On a Monday morning, a long time ago
The Chief of Police related a story
That of a criminal incident, a crime
Of a politically sensitive nature
Then sought my direction, counsel
On a course of action to take
To dispose of this criminal activity
At a party, over the weekend
In the city

An undercover police officer
Undoubtedly dressed as a civilian
For this important covert operation
Attending a party, hundred people or so
On a mission: searching for scofflaws
When he came across a city councilman
Smoking a joint, a refer, a marijuana cigarette
Not a good thing, that council member
Public official and all
The Chief bellowed "what should I do"
"How many other folks smoking joints" I snapped
"Many, many" the Chief responded
"How can we single out one" I quipped
Top which he deduced "good point"
"Must go after 'em all or none" case rests
At which time the caper ended
The Chief and his quest for justice and all
Or in this case, unequal justice for one

Another typical day in the city
Fighting crime; maintaining law, order
Another undercover convert operation
Handling difficult cases, solving crimes
Keeping the community safe for all
Using taxpayer dollars, protect the public
From one council member smoking a joint
Over the weekend, a typical weekend
In the city

The Bust!

A neighborhood kid, a typical punk
Videotaped by undercover police officers
From an indiscreet van, selling cocaine
Armed and dangerous, weapons and drugs
Caught red-handed, on tape for all to see
The evidence was clear, there must be a bust
His time was up, this punk, selling drugs
To other young folks, these users of cocaine
Making their "buys" in our city

This is not your typical bust, but a special occasion
This was the mayor's son, who must be arrested!
What should we do, how should we do it?
What special favor do we owe the mayor?
We must not run afoul of the district attorney!
These were the chief's thoughts, scared in a panic
Seeking a shield other than his badge, from me
For this sensitive bust, of this common drug dealer
Who just happened to be the mayor's drug dealer
Who just happened to be the mayor's son

We talked at length; reviewing our duties, options
What allegiance, courtesy, do we owe the mayor
Before, during, after; the bust of his son
Thought about courtesy call; the mayor would tell
Thought about a knock on the door; the kid would run
And finally, we agreed upon a plan that would work
Since we felt a special obligation, to do what was right
As his public servants, the public officials
Who owed a duty to all, for proper justice, this bust

The game plan was set, followed true to form
As the mayor's house was surrounded for the bust
With cops on all sides; by all doors, front and back
The officer in charge, lead cop, knocked on the door
Telling the mayor that his son was about to be had
The evidence in hand, quick action taken, this bust
Within minutes the scofflaw was caught, restrained

And brought to jail, booked, confined to a cell
So, he could later be brought to justice

The aftermath of our actions; fallout, ramifications
What would they be, how would they unfold?
After all, the mayor was still the mayor, for a while
Always felt I owed him some obligation, courtesy
To tell him in advance of the bust, the evidence
Animosity prevailed, the rest of his term
Ran next election, defeated, never sought office again
This nice mayor, bad son; doing my public duty
What was right for citizens; law, justice and all

The Political Sign

Political signs are regulated
In virtually all communities
Typically to limit their size
For a modicum of decorum
By all political candidates
During campaigns at election time

The sign size limit was four by four feet
Quite a simple rule to follow
But one candidate's sign, double this size
Twice the limit authorized by code
Must be reduced in size, now!
After all, it's the law

Notification took place, as required
Detailed instructions were provided
This scofflaw must correct his mistake
A fine is no option, there is no appeal
It's merely the law, which must be followed
By all candidate, plebe and seasoned alike

Low and behold!
Immediate compliance was the result
When the sign was cut in half
With one inch placed between the halves
Now two signs, both four by four feet
Those clever political candidate!

The candidate got elected to serve the people
Now he becomes an esteemed public official
A trusted member of the governing body
That must consider, adopt laws
To regulate political signs, one and all
For the good of the community!

The Three-Percent Solution

The democratic process unfolds, election time
The outcome of which, determined by the voters
In every city, it's the American way
Voting to elect our local public leaders
The process can be imperfect, sometimes is
For a variety of reasons, at least for one
It was payback time, by the cops, their union
Their chance to get back at the politicians

One typical year, cops got a three-percent raise
Salary increase that is, probably what they deserved
Given the cost-of-living at the time, low
And the economic hard times that prevailed, bad
This was approved, split vote of the governing body
Most of whom received less of a raise, their jobs
This was the rationale for their decision
To give the cops this three-percent raise

Happened by majority vote, the democratic way
The way it happens in all cities, these union contracts
Their decision stood, even though pressure to bear
Like pickets with signs, cops with their families
And numerous speakers with tales of woe
The impact of this paltry raise, their pocket-books
The city council stood fast, like they should
Waiting for the backlash; this police union
The following year, during the next election
This union got involved in the political process
Did they ever, with money and time, aplenty
As expected, the union endorsed the pro-cop candidates
They donated to their campaigns, union dues
And supported these folks in their off-duty time
By knocking on doors; making fliers, signs
Taking out newspaper ads, for their favorites

The outcome of the election was changed
Because of the police union, these political efforts
Anti-cop candidates out, pro-cop candidates in

And the next time raises came around, again
The cops got a fifteen-percent raise, payoff time
The union's politics worked, wonderfully well
They got what they wanted; made up for lost time
And the citizens had to foot the bill, these raises

After all, this was the American way, politicking
But wait, it ain't necessarily so, their involvement!
When you think that most cops lived elsewhere
Out of town, in other cities; not in this, their raise
Most of the cops did not even vote in the city
But merely came back to do their campaigning
And to make their soft-money contributions
To their favorite candidates, at election time

This outside force, union; police living elsewhere
Worked together to sway the local election
Greatly influencing the voters, the electorate
As they selected from candidates, their future leaders
Normally without the assistance of the cops
In their community, where they live, vote
Creating a dysfunctional democracy, this town,
Where most cops did not live, vote; only toiled for pay

Was this the democratic way, democracy at work?
Or merely a special interest group, wanting more pay!
Outside force, soft-money; this union with sway
Changing the outcome of this local election
You be the judge, was this the American way?
Or politics as usual, as it should be at election time
Perfectly legal, off-duty time, donations, and all
This special interest group, this union, these cops

Unions and Politics

I told the unions, but my advice did not hold sway
I told them not to back political candidates
But the unions prevailed, backing their favorites
Like they frequently do, seeking favors
From those candidates, who play to the unions
That employees place their hopes in
During those campaigns, at election time
For a larger pay raise, more benefits
Sometime in the future, based on their support

The leading mayoral candidate, against the unions
This was the base of his popular support
Among the blue-collar factory workers
And those seniors on fixed-incomes, retirees
The anti-government folks from both parties
Those citizens who wanted to hold government down
And do likewise with their property tax rates
These were the popular sentiments, held by most citizens
Throughout the town, at election time

The favorite mayoral candidate was always known
After all, the polls revealed it – must be true!
The underdog pandering to the unions
In an ill-fated attempt to gain the office
For which he was not elected by the people
The unsuccessful candidate could do nothing
For those poor unions, those enthusiastic backers
Who placed their hopes in a loser
During the campaign, at election time

The Advisory Body

Many years ago, balancing a budget
I recall the power of advisory bodies
Those citizens appointed to serve
To guide a particular municipal service
Like library, planning, parks and recreation
To evaluate proposals, program changes
Making recommendations to the body politic
On their particular service, department
This is common practice, everywhere

Before the public meeting on the budget
Coming back from lunch, I saw a flat-bed truck
Complete with a jazz band, straw hats and all
Handing out fliers, yelling, detailing the impact
Of planned budget cuts for the library
These members of the library board
And their partners, the friends of the library
Drumming up public support, against the cuts
Soon to be considered by the city council

The mayor opened the public meeting
Speaker after speaker spoke, against the cuts
Saying that children would have no place to go
That juvenile delinquency would be on the rise
That crime would increase in neighborhoods
This would be the impact, those library cuts
Planned by the city council, to balance the budget
After the public hearing; the debate, the vote
Not to cut these library services at all

Upon reflection, an important conclusion
That criminals must use library services
Since if reduced, crime would increase
This public hearing made a definite point
The power of citizen advisory groups
Those built-in advocates for their service
The service they are there to serve
And protect against budget cuts
From those who must balance the budget

The Analyst

Hired to analyze, to be objective
To provide impartial recommendations
That assists when making important decisions
The elected officials, the governing body
On those complicated issues, analysis required
The way it should be, for the body politic
When making important decisions
For the citizens, on their behalf
By these ultimate holders of the public trust
This is the job of the analyst

One of the analyst's first assignments
Analyzing the need for a rate increase
For an important cab company, the largest
Flag drop fees, mileage rates, waiting time charges
Even the cost of placing bags in the trunk, by piece
Of these cabs, providers of portal-to-portal service
Save the limousine and the driver
Important factors to analyze, objectivity a must
For these requested rate increases

Many hours of analysis, important recommendation
From the staff, the advisors to the city council
The recommendation was clear, fully documented
The rates sought exceeded the cost-of-living
Some customers "locked" into these cab services
Such as senior citizens, the handicapped, the poor
Many of whom are on fixed incomes
Recommended a more modest adjustment
With discounts for these special groups
Waited for the debate, the vote, the outcome

The decision was quick, decisive, without hesitation
The motion was made, unanimously approved
For this cab company, and their owners
Who always gave to the local politicians
At every election time, with the expectation
Of a favorable consideration

On their requested rate increases
The staff only advisory, the democratic way
When making important decisions
By the representatives of the people

Moving the Hookers

There was a time, not long ago
On a street, in a city, out West
Where there were dozens, scores of hookers
All parading on the street, strutting their stuff
Making eye contact, potential johns in passing cars
Waiting to cut a deal, make a buck
Sun, rain, hot cold; inclement weather notwithstanding
Quite a resilient group, these hookers!

City government can't stand for that
It's against the law, public morals, common decency
Especially if they are parading in front
Of your house or place of business
Not good for the neighborhood, commerce
Property values, community pride, and all
Especially for families, let alone children
These hookers on the street

Cops must move the hookers, it's their job
Day after day, night after night, year after year
Away from the homes, the businesses
Like squeezing a balloon, metaphorically
They go from one place to another, any other
An occasional bust; removed, out in an hour
Temporary displacement, migration, at best
Their numbers never seem to decrease

They only, always, seem to relocate
Cops rough them up, move them out!
To another street, in another neighborhood
Maybe another town, if we're lucky
Where their cops do the same, with equal vigor
In this endless battle to remove the hookers
From one street, neighborhood, city, to another
To again strut their stuff, looking for johns

Rear Window

I look out my window at City Hall
And see citizens coming and going
Many to pay their taxes, some to complain
Some to pay their taxes and complain
The process continues all day long
Day-in and day-out, year after year
This hustle-and-bustle at City Hall

As I look across the street from my window
I see hookers strutting their stuff, on display
Looking for johns to turn a trick, make a buck
I see cars stopping; negotiations take place
Deals re cut; meeting-of-the-minds
Then the cars go on their way
The hooker is gone, only to return another day

Strange how some people pay taxes
On their personal property, assets
That they sometimes seldom use
While others use their personal property
Oftentimes quite frequently, these assets
Below the level of awareness, concern
And don't pay any taxes at all

It's been a long-standing practice
For cities to levy property taxes
On the immovable, the unhideable
Things that are there for everyone to see
While others move their property about quietly
Sometimes barely visible to the naked eye
And don't pay any taxes at all!

The Law Firm

The big law firm, one of the largest
And the most prestigious
In the entire state, region
Their partners ivy leaguers, one and all
Making bid donations, contributions
Generally, to the incumbents
With the goal of continuing their services
Special, general, bond counsels, more
Based on their reputation, competence?
Or merely the fact they gave a donation
To the politicians
Who vote for their services
After election time
In the city

LESSON SIX

PERSONAL REFLECTIONS

A Boy's Dream!

When I was just a boy
Living out in the country
Out in the sticks with the hicks
And longing for the city
To visit the downtown
When I was just a boy
With but a dream

I would sneak downtown
By myself all alone
Hitchhiking all the way
Against parental wishes
And adult common sense
To visit the city
And its downtown

I can remember the experience now
From the downtown, center of the city
Those sights, sounds, an

smells
The individuals that make up the people
And the buildings tha t define the architecture
In the center of the city
In the "guts" of its downtown

What a place!
When I was just a boy
Living in the country
And longing for the city
To visit the downtown
When I was just a boy
With but a dream

Opening Packages

I dream of cities in faraway lands
Of cities that I may never see
I dream of cities in faraway lands
Of cities that I shall never see
Of cities I know I will not see

I have seen cities in many lands
Housing major populations of the world
These geopolitical packages of societies
Each package awaiting to be opened
By the exploring spirit

I must dream of these cities
And these packages awaiting to be opened
In these cities of the world
Awaiting the exploring spirit
Especially from citizens like myself

My Favorite Things

I like cities built by the best nature has to offer!
Like oceans, harbors, bays, ports, rivers, and lakes

I like the unique architecture of our cities!
Their institutions, commercials buildings, and residential structures

I like the parks and open spaces in our cities!
With their monuments, fountains, bandstands, and playgrounds

I like the unique neighborhoods in our cities!
With their inherent cultures, customs, and peoples

I like the common traditions in our cities!
What goes on in their parks, bandstands, and open spaces

I like the various groups of people in our cities!
Those people that bring life to a neighborhood

These are a few of the things I like about cities!
That make them meaningful, enjoyable to me

This holds true for America's cities!
As well as cities throughout the world

The Internet

I have seen many cities from cyberspace
On the internet, watching my computer screen
Their natural amenities, man-made monuments
Their architecture from a time gone by
Their public infrastructure, their . . .
From these pictures available on my screen
At home, on the internet

I long to experience, for real, first-hand
Those aspects of cities that I can never see
From cyberspace, on the internet
Like their people, their foods; scents
Neighborhoods, parks, public places
The dynamics of their everyday living
The lives of people I wish I could meet

As I dream of cities in faraway lands
Cities I know I will never see
Any day soon; maybe never, ever
Except from cyberspace, over the internet
So many cities, so little time
I dream of cities far away, anyway
I dream of these cities, almost everyday

Cities: The Highs and Lows

Cities
Centers of our society
Of the arts, entertainment, architecture
The location of business and commerce
And government agencies, services
Mass-transit and people movers
The dynamic interchange of all
The apex of our civilization
Our windows to the world

Cities
Home of immigrants and refugees
Refuse for the destitute
Providing shelters for the homeless
And food kitchens for the poor
For those who don't fit in neatly with society
Who have problems society must resolve
Our windows to the world

Cities
The reality of America
These highs and lows
Of greatness and despair
Side-by-side, these extremes
That exist in our cities
Causing middle-class flight; suburbs
With the lows following right behind

Culture v. Counterculture

Culture!
The state of the arts, literature, religion, philosophy
Of social development and work skills too
For a given people, certain period of time
A society has culture, expressed in cities
By those people residing there, living daily
The citizens demonstrate these qualities
These characteristics of what we call culture
Cities are the windows of our culture
For all the world to see

Counterculture!
Society refers to the opposite of culture
Those citizens that represent and demonstrate
Different views, thoughts, and actions
In the arts, literature, religion, and philosophy
And in their social development, work skills too
That run counter to mainstream society, norms
Those in the minority, not in the popular culture
As the majority would like to have it considered
These people represent the counterculture

The counterculture can also become the culture
As popular views and actions change over time
And come to represent the mainstream, norms
About what people think is their culture
As this group of people becomes larger
The counterculture becomes the culture
And people with other different views, norms, emerge
That come to represent the counterculture anew
And this is how it goes in society, culture v. counterculture
By the residents of our cities, with the passage of time

Vanishing Differences

The regional differences in our cities
They are quickly disappearing, vanishing
Thanks to mega-franchisers, national chains
And all those publicly-held corporations
That dot our urban landscape
Like honey bees in a hive

They do not adapt, they superimpose
Their uniform goods and services
That don't embrace history, tradition
They invade our buildings, and
While the architecture remains the same
Regional differences go, nowhere to be found

The many unique differences, characteristics
Where have they all gone, where will they go
As they are melded together by these corporate giants
These monolithic providers of goods and services
That make our cities the same in many ways
They must be held accountable for their actions!

Movers and Shakers

America's cities
Home of the movers and the shakers
Home of the moven and the shaken
Both groups occupy our cities
Sometimes side-by-side
And in great numbers
These dichotomous groups
The extremes of our society
In America's cities

Roots

A tree in the forest
When its roots become damaged
And it temporarily loses its footing
Is held up by the neighboring trees
Those stronger than itself
Until it reestablishes its roots
And regains its footing
And can again stand on its own
Just like it should be for people
People living in our cities

Roadways

I have traveled to many cities
On the interstates, highways, and freeways
But seldom the local roadways
Or the backroads
Have I really seen the cities?
Have I really seen their people?

To see the cities, their people
You must get off of the interstates, highways, and freeways
And take the local roadways
The backroads
To see the cities
And their people

Interstates, highways, and freeways
Are good to view geography, the landscape
To get from point "a" to point "b"
To save time
But not to see the cities
And their people

You may travel many roads only once
As you go through life's short journey
So, stay off the interstates, highways, and freeways
And take the local roadways
The backroads
See the cities
And their people

The Culinary Arts

Across America, throughout the land
Our cuisine is becoming uniform, standard
For breakfast, lunch, and dinner
From city to city, place to place
Almost without exception
Like the national culture

The exact same thing, different places
Thanks for fast-food chains, one and all
That spread relentlessly, continually
Like a cancer on the urban landscape
From coast to coast, state to state
Permeating our neighborhoods, every block

Spreading culinary blandness, sameness
Eliminating preferences, regional differences
And those special foods, unusual places
That we've had special foods at these unusual places
Have dropped like flies in recent times
Never to show their place or plate again

Starting now and into the future
Our children will know no culinary differences
As they become accustomed, programmed
To frequenting those fast-food restaurants
Those chains that bind the cities in our nation
And restrict our culinary options, forever

Prices Citizens Pay

In our cities, not long ago
Use to be that every item had a price tag
And, at a glance, you know what it cost
Pretty much the same for all goods and services
Throughout the years, in our cities

Nowadays prices seem to change constantly
Demand pricing is now the trend to follow
With "peak-time" pricing everywhere
And prices based on the season of the year
Along with month of year, week of the month

And by day, hour of the day around the corner
With minutes and seconds to follow
Combined with weekend specials, holiday packages
Early bird dinners, movies, late night discounts too
Off-peak and off-season rates abound

These are the prices of things
Of the goods and services
Available to the citizens in our cities
That very depending on a hundred variables
Seems like from all businesses. in every town

Downside of the Military

Military bases are a necessary evil
Readying young men for war
To protecting our way of life
Their members serving their time
Going to town in their off-duty hours
Creating markets for goods and services
Which are catered to by the local merchants
Trying to satisfy their every need, whim
These young men serving their country

Hitchhiking to the big city, downtown
When I was a boy, a child of the suburbs
Longing to see the action of downtown
Here I saw the downside of the military
The side most people don't see
The side tucked away in seedy corners
Taking place on the dark streets, alleys
In out-of-the-way places, in cheap rented spaces
Providing the goods and services they desired

I can remember it well, indelibly
Like it was yesterday, four decades later
Those skinheads in civilian clothes
Made important by serving their country
Trying to be someone, in their own way
For away from home, without a home
Doing their military service, time
Their duty for their country, the USA
Like their fathers had done before them

I vividly recall the merchandise, services
That served their needs, this group
The myriad locker clubs, tattoo parlors
Frequent girlie bars and topless places
Numerous peep shows, X-rated movie theaters
The girls, women, catering to their needs
On the street, in dark places, little spaces

Away from the spotlight of downtown
Not far from these military bases

And the other businesses of like trade
Such as the pool halls, dance palaces
Those inexpensive cafes, bowling alleys
The petty amusement parks, penny arcades

And cheap jewelry stores a plenty
With rings for girls, and lay-away plans
All operating in a limitless seamy market
This was all downtown, way down town
All serving the downside of the military

Military Towns

Some girls go downtown
Looking for guys, boyfriends, beaus
With romance and love in mind
Wanting to escape their home life
Their blue-collar existence
Seeking social commitments, long-term
In all the wrong places, from the wrong people
That's why some girls go downtown

Some guys go downtown too
Looking for some touch, opposite sex
Physical attraction, sex in mind
Affection and romance not required
Wanting to escape their lonely existence
Or life in the military, on the base
That's why some guys go downtown
Seeking these girls in all the right places

No matchmakers delight
These unusual couples, coupling
Just people passing the night
At bars, dance halls, night clubs
Each trying to find what they want
In the military town at night
Seeking commitments for different reasons
Based on friendships of acquaintance

Sex in the City

You can find anything you want
Satisfy your most intimate desires
If you know how to shop, in the city
Retail or wholesale, cash or credit
It's always for sale, somewhere downtown
Available from some sources, for a fee
Sought by many customers, at a cost
Always at a fee, based on supply and demand
Details negotiated up front, acts to follow
That's how you buy sex, in the city

It's all there, for sale, to fit any sexual desire
From heterosexuals, homosexuals, bisexuals
Even trans-gender, cross-gender, multi-gender
Those with no gender, or just confused ones
Old, young; male, female; in all sizes and colors
Active, passive; overt, covert; whatever you want
Special techniques, multiple techniques
To satisfy any individual preference, fetish
Or no particular specialty at all, it's all there
With only the cost, place, to be determined

Happens in places a plenty, take your pick
In cars and vans, in back rooms, in cheap hotels
There's always a place to make brief contact
Especially in dark places, out of the way spaces
By people selling themselves to strangers in the night
These people of a similar preference, sometimes fate
Determined by nature, possibly by design, happenstance
They can be alone to hate, despise, what they do
What they have come to be, their being
In these dark places, in the city, with strangers

Evolution of the Computer

During the 1970's
Almost every city had a mainframe computer
Its functions limited: data processing
For the finance department, its applications
Payroll, budget, billing, collections
In all cities, it was the way it was, then
Mini-computer, where they existed, few
Used by engineers: technical applications
This was the use of computers, software
The finance department was king
This is how it was, during the 1970's

During the 1980's
Hardware and software revolution taking place
No need to be an expert, know programming
Or to develop your own applications, any kind
Hardware smaller, less expensive, more available
Software simpler, more user friendly, anyone can use
New applications evolving; everywhere, real-time
To be used by everyone; secretaries, clerks too
Department managers demanding their due
From these micro-computers, packaged software
This is how it was, during the 1980's

During the 1990's
Computers and software everywhere, even at home
Cheaper, more user friendly; all want to use, cities too
Standard applications available, all departments
Need to take control away from finance, only their needs
Who traditionally had responsibility for such things
Throughout the decades, over the years, in all cities
Management information systems, information technology
Should be available, all departments, top on down
The computer hardware, software, devolution took place
This how it was during the 1990s'

Perspectives

You can observe planet earth from a satellite
Different countries can be viewed from an airplane
One can see various states from their automobile
You can even see a city from your car
But you must walk in the city to experience it
You must live in a city to know its neighborhoods
To become friends with its people
There is no short-cut, no other way
To truly experience a city

LESSON SEVEN

CLOSING THOUGHTS

Still Dreaming!

When I was young
I'd look at maps, with their cities
Whishing I could see them all
When I was just a boy
When I was just a boy
Dreaming of places, I've never been
Dreaming of cities, I hoped to see

As time passed
I saw cities, some of them
First by foot, then by bike
Then by hitchhiking, finally by car
Then by plane, some in foreign lands
Making my dreams come true
Dreams of cities

Now that I am older
I look at maps, with their cities
Wishing that I'd have seen more
Still dreaming of cities, I haven't seen
Places I've never been
Still dreaming of cities
Still dreaming of cities!

Man v. Nature

The battle began long ago
That of man versus nature
City versus country, urban versus rural
For many years nature prevailed
Forests, wilderness, waterways
Things were natural, man adapted
Nature prevailed

Man began to clear nature; to build, develop
Villages, boroughs, towns, then cities
Eating away at nature, making room
For the buildings, streets, parking lots
By cutting away the forests, wildernesses
And by altering nature's waterways
All done for the sake of "progress"?

Now our cities are asphalt, steel, concrete
With little space reserved for nature
Except small pockets of parks, open spaces
Where people go to get away; must get away
From the congestion, noise, life in the city
But so many people, so little nature
People began to question "progress"?

Man appears to be winning the battle
But losing the war, the war against nature
The more nature disappears
The more citizens demand its presence
Those who live on man-made urban heat islands
Mostly devoid of nature, these cities
Built under the auspices of "progress"?

Judging a City

People should judge a city, any city
Not by the extent of its economic affluence
But, rather, how it treats its lowest members
The unemployable, unemployed, underemployed
Those with mental and physical ailments
Those with addictions, afflictions
Those who are homeless, hungry
These are the lowliest members of a city

How are these citizens treated?
Are you proud of the service they are provided?
Are you satisfied with the care they are receiving?
Do these services provide the proper cycle for healing?
How does your city fare?
Does your city even care?
Any city!
America's cities!

The Democratic Way?

Is it the will of the people
Those votes expressed through the ballot
Curing elections, at election time
Those citizens selecting their leaders
With agendas for the future
Satisfying the needs of their constituents
The majority of citizens, some of the people
At least the fifty-one percent
Is this the democratic way?

Is it not the true goal of the majority
To accommodate the minority
The other forty-nine percent
Although not a requirement of democracy
It is the humane and politically civil thing to do
To create harmony in the community
When setting the agenda for the future
For all of the citizens, all of the people
Not just the simple majority

What is the true mandate of the politicians?
The purpose of the body politic?
To ignore and alienate the minority
Or create electoral harmony among all
And peace in the community with many
Democracy can be designed to embrace
Both the franchised and disenfranchised alike
And not just the fifty-one percent
This is the role of a caring democracy

The political system can be designed
To accommodate all of the people
Not merely the majority of the people
This is the mark of a caring community leader
And the hallmark of an astute body politic
That no single group should hold sway
But that important decisions be made
To satisfy all citizens of the community
Not just the fifty-one percent!

Our Architecture

The architecture of the city
For many years, throughout the years
Displayed steeples, spires, domes, and copulas
Representing the most important institutions
Architectural showcases of the community

The buildings they rested upon included
Houses of worship, seats of government
Educational institutions, financial centers
The most important institutions
In the life of citizens in the community

The architectural landscape has changed
The steeples, spires, domes, and copulas
Have all but disappeared, made insignificant
By new man-made monuments on the cityscape
Testimonials to the private sector

These monuments to the corporate world
Now built by the lowest bidders
Primarily of concrete and steel
High-rise structures housing cubicle offices
And residential bird cages for citizens

The old architectures are all but gone
With the passage of time, over the years
For it is cheaper to build anew
Rather than restore these antiquities
In our cities throughout the land

Monuments No More

Out public buildings use to be monuments
Monuments to things greater than man
Providing halls of government
Housing seats of governance
And sacred democratic processes
These unique American institutions
In these old public buildings
That provided the historical landscape
Of our cities

Now they're built by the lowest bidder
Cutting corners to save a buck
Designed to bring projects in on-time, under-budget
They serve their purpose
No monuments to our legacy
None intended
In our new public buildings
That provide the contemporary urban landscape
Of our cities

Our Urban Islands

America's inner-city cores need help
These man-made urban heat islands
They need services and programs
For all categories of human beings
Yet few governments, people, seem to care
Or give the time or the money to assist
To improve the lot of their fellow citizens
In these cities with the best and the brightest

That host our finest educational institutions
Where services and programs go wanting
If the educated, the elite, are not compassionate
Who will be, will anyone be, will no one be
I went to the big city, looking for America
And I could not find it anywhere, no where
Which leads me to believe, most certainly
That most citizens aren't busy being born again

They are dying like those inner-city cores
Those man-made urban heat islands
The very guts of our largest cities
Our showplaces to the nation, the world
Where visitors come to see America
And can't find it anywhere, especially there
Because people aren't busy being born again
They're dying like our inner cities

America's Main Streets

During my travels, over the years
I have seen many a Main Street in decay
Having been left unattended to wither away
Left on their own throughout the years
These Main Streets in America's cities
Where my parents went on Saturday night

I have witnessed many effort to revitalize them
With their different streetscapes and landscapes
And their public places and open spaces
All designed to bring businesses and people
Back to Main Street, like it used to be
Like it had been in the past, in a time gone by

Some of these plans work; but most don't
These futile efforts to renew our Main Streets
With their partial streetscapes and landscapes
And marginal public places and open spaces
These plans done at City Hall in a vacuum
These quick-fix efforts by politicians

And when these plans have worked
They were designed with the people in mind
The people that want to go without fear
Where their parents went before them
That special place in the center of town
To experience life on their Main Street

Recipe for Renewal

Deterioration takes place before decay
Decay always happens before renewal
Cities are no exception
Citizens cannot expect renewal
Unless a feeling of rebirth and pride take place
Among the citizens themselves
In the city, any city

A city cannot expect private investment
Unless, and until, it invests in itself first
The recipe is similar from city to city
Regardless of its size
Its geographic location
Or its form of government
The citizens must demand this action
From their elected leaders

The ingredients of the recipe are the same
An adequate public infrastructure is number one
Followed by a restoration of public buildings
And the allocation of parks, open spaces for all
These come first, before private investment
A city must invest in itself first
This the citizens must demand

Private investment will follow
Economic incentives may help
But a feeling of rebirth and pride
Are most important, vital
Among the people, their elected leaders
In the recipe for renewal
For America's cities

The Workers

One of the most important functions of cities
Entrusted to the employees of public works
Those laborers, truck drivers, mechanics
The maintainers of the public infrastructure
And the municipal vehicular fleet
This function is the same for all cities
Regardless of size or geographic location
That of public works

These workers, one city, primarily African-American
Same workers, another city, primarily Mexican-American
In yet another city, primarily Polish-American
Those laborers, truck drivers, mechanics
The maintainers of the public infrastructure
And the municipal vehicular fleet
The employees of public works
The bedrock of municipal services

In the future these demographics will change
As the offspring of these employees
Become better educated, seek the American Dream
Of doing better, being better off, than their fathers were
And don't forget those women entering the workforce
Their future will be different than the past
Among the employees of public works
In your city, my city – one day in all cities

Buzz Words

People place to much faith in buzz words
And what they purport to represent
Including elected officials, citizens too
And especially students, learning from books
They try to equate these buzz words, phrases
With sound management practices
Don't blame them, they don't know the difference

In my generation alone, there's been many
I first began reading, hearing about them, in school
Then from highly-paid private consultants
Sometimes reading about them in magazines
These fancy words and phrases, catchers of attention
That sometimes even make the press
Especially when used by high-ranking public officials

I recall some of the fancier words and phrases
Such as planning, programming, budgeting systems
Then there was zero-base and performance budgeting
Don't forget privatization and benchmarking
And of course, there is no planning without
One of the newest buzzwords, strategic planning
The list goes on, and is constantly changing

As any good seasoned manager knows
These buzzwords represent merely techniques
Are not end states unto themselves; panaceas
They are merely tools available to the manager
Tools for a specific purpose, management aids
And the best managers are those
With many tools in their tool box

Lo is the manager with but a few tools
Or the one that only uses the latest techniques
And thinks he or she is state-of-the-art
These are not managers, managing
They are merely bureaucrats, pseudo-managers
With empty tool boxes, trying to impress
When they manage with buzz words

Loyalty v. Competency

In some of America's cities
Those with the strong-mayor form of government
Jobs at the highest levels are filled with people
Frequently based on loyalty, not competency
Or worse yet, political party affiliation
For the strong mayor, the elected chief executive
Desires loyalty, similar party politics, above all
When filling jobs and performing duties
In the city halls, our municipal corporations
Those cities with this type of governance

In most of America's cities
Those with a trained professional manager
Who are hired because they are the best and the brightest
Jobs at the highest levels are always filled
Based solely on competency, never loyalty
With total disregard to political party affiliation
For the professional manager, above all else
Desires competency when filling jobs, performing duties
For the citizens who pay their taxes
To run city hall like a private corporation

As a taxpayer which do you prefer?
To run your municipal government, your corporation
With employees hired based on their loyalty
And their political party affiliation
Or those hired based on their competency alone
The best and the brightest, who serve all equally
When doing the jobs for the taxpayers
The stockholders of the corporation
Who wish their leaders to serve as directors
Like the finest private corporations

What's in a Name?

The name "bureaucrat" is merely a word
As a noun it describes a person, place, thing
A person without a face, human qualities
Who works in a place called government, bureaucracy
Dealing with things bureaucratic, red tape
Those rules and regulations that must be enforced
By those who you call a bureaucrat

Citizens do not like bureaucrats
For they represent the last problem
Their last encounter, negative interface
With government; at any and all levels
The name of the person you don't know
Who told you the rules you must follow
Or that you couldn't do what you wanted

Hey you, citizen, I am the bureaucrat!
The child from the blue-collar family
The kid on the block who joined the military
The adult who went to school on the G.I. bill
The suitor who married your daughter
The parent who raised his kids to be good citizens
The family man who is your neighbor

I am the bureaucrat!
The one you've been calling this name
All these years, over the decades
Please put a face with the name
The whole person with this term
A real life with this negative title
A whole family with this noun

For I am what you call a bureaucrat
Who does my best to serve you
And all citizens equally, unequivocally
I am a bureaucrat, I am this bureaucrat
And I'm proud of it!
Damn proud of it!
And don't you forget it!

Old Bureaucrat!

The sage asked the aging bureaucrat about his life
After a long career of serving cities, the people in them
Ol' bureaucrat, what have you done for humanity
After your many long years of public service
In the city, your cities; the ones you've served
And spent most of your life, these cities
What parting thoughts can you impart,
About the impact your life has had on others
Oh, speak to me about your life's work
Your contributions after these many years
In those cities in which you've spent your time
Your entire life, ol' bureaucrat
Tell me of your life's accomplishments

Oh wise one, reflecting upon my life, I can say
I've had no impact on humanity like great philosophers
I've had no impact on civilization like great scholars
I've had no impact on society like great leaders
But my life's work has not been in vain, not a waste
For I have had a respectful impact on communities
Those cities where I have had the honor to work
The privilege of serving their leaders, helping citizens
In many various ways of which I feel proud.
Of making life better for other human beings
Those citizens in these cities, communities
In which I have labored long hours, over many years
Throughout our Great Land

I remember the public services I helped to initiate
Those programs for young folks and for senior citizens
The services for the alienated and the disadvantaged
Those for the poor, as well as their families
I recall those times I've helped maintain services, vital ones
To improve the quality of life, character of the community
The many times I've helped to hold down taxes
Devised and designed innovative programs with limited funds
Did my best to revitalize, reinvigorate downtowns
Recommended sound solutions on major policy issues

The many times governing bodies have followed my heed
Resolving sensitive political issues, the public unaware
That helped to make the city a better place to live, work

I've had an impact on cities, albeit not many, and
Feel proud of my accomplishments of helping others
All segments of the community over many years
These deeds, while not great acts, make a life well spent
My family, wife and children, lived in these cities
My children were raised in these communities
Those where I've worked, spent my life, toiled these years
Working with their leaders and citizens of all kinds
My impact on humanity, and, society, not great
But my impact on the city, community, was admirable
This ol' bureaucrat has lived a worthwhile life
In those cities where I've worked, lived, aged
Helping to improve government for others

After a long silence, the sage, upon reflection, responded
Ol' bureaucrat, you've had a life of many accomplishments
Of which you should be proud, these cities, you've worked
Do not worry about your impact on humanity
Civilization, society, for you have helped people
Community leaders, those cities in which you toiled
Life is a better place for citizens because of your actions
The decisions you've made to improve the workings
The operations of those governments where you've served
Your impact has been measurable, lasting, and
Has helped pave the way for others who have followed you
In their efforts to serve elected leaders and citizens
For these achievements you should be proud

The Big Picture

I've worked in cities, nearly a quarter century
First employed to analyze their operation, their parts
Then hired by elected officials, by majority vote
To manage their functions, their departments
Reorganizations, downsizing, streamlining, automation
Modernizing staff departments, central management too
Managing the managers; responsible for their hiring, firing
In charge of these important functions of bureaucracy
Of these complex municipal organizations
That provide a multitude of services to the public
Keeping them efficient, effective, lean-and-mean machines
That's been my job over all these years
In those few cities in which I have worked, spent my life

I should know cities, their big picture, but don't
Only the ones in which I've worked, over my short career
Know their functions, operations, how to manage them
The components of their government, their process of governance
The guts of their departments, services, programs, projects
But don't really know about cities; their essence
Don't really know about their essence at all
About their unique characteristics, their casual patterns
Their reason for being, their tempo of activity, pace of life
Of their sidewalks, streets, neighborhoods, public places
Let alone the social fabric of the community
With its ethnic enclaves of racial and cultural diversity
I don't really know these qualities at all

I wish I knew these aspects of cities
For to really know a city, all cities, any city
You must live in it, work in it, play in it
Walk on its sidewalks, drive on its streets, meet its people
Visit its many neighborhoods, parks, public places
Know their monuments, their history, reason for being
Getting to know cities is like knowing people
Cities are part of the crowd, unless you single one out
To spend part of your life there, to live there

This is the only way to truly know a city
And its place in society, history, how it fits in
To the landscape of America's cities, the big picture
You must live a part of your life there, in the city

LESSON EIGHT

THE FUTURE

Societal Changes and Municipal Public Services

Roger L. Kemp, PhD

Societal Changes

Societal changes in Canada and the United States are having a dramatic impact on the types and levels of municipal public services being provided by cities to their citizens in recent years. The impacts of these societal changes on a local government's public services are highlighted below. These services are provided by public officials to their citizens, the taxpayers that they serve. The following major societal changes are used to describe their impact on the municipal public services that are presently being provided by local governments throughout these nations, including evolving and changing public services.

- ➤ More sophisticated computer hardware systems and software applications
- ➤ Citizens can increasingly acquire information about their city from its website without having to visit city hall
- ➤ New computer software programs, such as Wi-Fi, GIS, and GPS can be used to improve the level of public services, as well as to enhance economic development
- ➤ Easier public access, via online resources, to elected and appointed officials
- ➤ The influx of immigrant members to a city's population creates new demands for public services
- ➤ Recent economic hard-times creates a need for additional revenues
- ➤ More sophisticated video recording systems are now being used to videotape public meetings, and shown them online to citizens
- ➤ The changing nature of families, with both parents of children frequently working full-time
- ➤ The aging U.S. population has expanded the demand for senior citizen services
- ➤ The focus on school safety has led to new school security and educational programs
- ➤ Many municipal departments now have equal access to new computer software programs to enhance the quality of their public services
- ➤ Increasingly 24-7 access is available for citizens to seek information about their public services, their municipal organization, copies of public documents, and to email their public officials

Impact on Public Services

These societal changes have influenced, impacted, and created the following public services. These services are highlighted below in alphabetical order, except for the first entry, which provides an overview of general public service changes. The following list includes: General Public Services, City Clerk Services, Economic Development Services, Educational Services, Financial Services,

Fire Services, Health Services, Human Resources Services, Information Technology Services, Library services, Parks and Recreation Services, Planning and Building Services, Police Services, and Public Works Services. The impacts of these societal changes are felt by citizens on a daily basis in the cities that they live in.

General Public Services

- There are many more sophisticated municipal websites online for citizens to access
- In the olden days mayor's typically had a toll-free telephone number, now they have an email address listed on their city's website
- Other elected officials, such as city council members, and other public officials, also have their email address listed on their city's website
- Public services are being adapted and provided to serve and meet the needs of recent immigrant citizens
- More frequent adjustments to departmental user fees and charges are being made
- There is an increase in joint purchasing. Many cities can now purchase common products and services from their county and state government websites
- Nowadays many municipal user fees and charges can frequently be paid online with a credit card
- An increased usage is being made for Wi-Fi (wireless computer networks) in cities throughout the country

City Clerk Services

- Many public documents are now made available online to citizens
- Videos of public meetings are commonly available on municipal websites, as well as local public access cable television channels
- More licenses, permits, and fees can now be applied and paid for online on municipal websites
- The agendas of public meetings of elected and appointed officials are now available on these websites, as well as the minutes from their previous meetings
- The agendas of board and commission meetings are now commonly available online on municipal websites, as are the minutes from their previous meetings as well.
- Frequently, vacancies for board and commission appointments are advertised online to solicit citizen involvement on their city's boards and commissions

Economic Development Services

- Geographic Information Systems (GIS) make available information about a community that may stimulate economic development
- Such information includes age levels, incomes, and information about citizens based on the geographic areas within a community

- It also shows the commercial areas, as well as the population densities, of a community's various geographic areas
- This information also includes the location of sewer and water lines, and other public utilities, that are available to serve properties – both developed and undeveloped
- Funds from higher levels of government are typically available to redevelop "brownfield" sites, contaminated sites that must be cleaned before they can be developed
- An increasing number of municipal building and zoning regulation ordinances are now available online for the public to access
- The increased use of Wi-Fi networks is being made on Main Streets and in downtown areas to promote economic development by attracting more citizens who like to use their computers when they eat meals, snacks, and drink coffee

Educational Services

- An increasing number of schools are offering full-day pre-school and kindergarten programs, since the parents of school children are increasingly both working full-time
- Many schools are now using electronic textbooks since they are easy to access, less expensive, and reduce the weight of a student's backpack
- Schools are increasingly using email and text message notifications of school cancellations, early dismissals, and other selected important events
- Many schools are now placing their students class assignments online, and parents can access them to make sure that their students are doing their homework
- More anti-drug educational programs and services are now being provided to students
- The use of school security programs and services are increasing

Financial Services

- More frequent adjustments to departmental user fees and charges
- Most department managers, as well as their employees, can access their respective budgets online 24-7 throughout the year
- Many coordinated team efforts to save funds from the current approved budget to offset a projected deficit for the coming fiscal year are now common
- Management increasingly works with employee organizations to focus on ways to save money to avoid laying off employees to balance future budgets
- Increased coordination of joint purchasing programs with other local and regional governments, as well as respective state/provincial governments
- The development of online payment systems to facilitate the payment of property taxes by citizens
- More municipal financial information is available online for citizens to review (e.g., annual budgets, both proposed and approved, annual audits, as well as information about the current budget process).

Fire Services

- Computers on fire trucks assist in providing information when fire fighters respond to calls-for-service (e.g., on-site chemicals, the location of fire hydrants, and the structural layout of the property), which are now known before the response is made
- These computer data bases are available at the main department's office and are continually being updated to provide this on-site information to their fire employees
- Many cities have established Emergency Operations Centers (EOC's) to address inclement weather and/or emergency management incidents, and related issues, to provide up-to-date information on these issues to their citizens

Health Services

- More health-related educational programs are being provided to senior citizens
- A greater number of physical fitness workshops are being provided to senior citizens
- More quit-smoking classes are being provided to senior citizens
- Many educational programs and services are being provided to reduce childhood obesity
- Health-related literature is commonly being made available to citizens of all ages
- Some services, such as inoculations and medications, are now being made available to the general public
- Communities are providing more dental clinics to senior citizens, since this service is not covered by Medicare

Human Resources Services

- Citizens can increasingly apply for municipal jobs online on their city's website
- All of a city's approved labor agreements are available, typically online, for employees and citizens to access, to determine approved salaries and fringe benefits
- Increasingly, the risk management programs have been transferred to the human resources function
- Most personnel documents, including those listing employee contacts, employment applications, and related city policies (e.g., such as nepotism policies) are available online

Information Technology Services

- State-of-the-art websites are increasingly commonplace in local governments
- More sophisticated hardware and software are being provided organization-wide
- All departments are being treated equally from a computer hardware and software standpoint
- Sometimes organization-wide Departmental User Committees are formed to ensure that all departments functions are being properly served from an IT standpoint

- Social media is increasingly being used by public officials to announce municipal events and services to the public
- Access to Wi-Fi networks is increasingly being provided in downtown areas to attract citizens and to enhance economic development in these areas

Library Services

- Additional electronic devices including computers, tablets, and e-book readers are being made available for adults, youth, and children to use
- More computer classes are being offered to citizens of all ages
- Some computer classes are being offered in the foreign language of recent immigrant populations
- Touch-screens and educational software is being provided for children to use
- More available online resources are being made available to citizens of all ages
- Fewer reference books and periodicals are now being used, since many are now available online
- Larger collections of educational and entertainment media (music and film) in CD and DVD formats due to increased public demand
- Digital collections of books, recordings, and films are being made available for library users to download to their personal online devices (may eventually replace CD's and DVD's)
- Printing and scanning equipment is available for library users of all ages
- Most citizens have 24-7 access to their library's online library resources and services
- An increased number of community services are now available, such as tax preparation workshops, evening presentations on relevant topics, information on health-related services, and the free-use of library space for non-profit community organizations to use for their programs and meetings
- There is an increasing demand for small study spaces for individuals and small groups to work, study, and/or use available Wi-Fi services
- Use of social networks (Facebook, Twitter, Instagram, etc.) to not only share information between the library and its users about programs and topics of interest, but also to facilitate a dialog, are being used
- The increased use of online newsletters with the ability to target individual interests, and inform citizens of all ages of the services and resources available from their library

Parks and Recreation Services

- The expansion of lunch programs at Senior Citizens Centers
- The increased number of handicraft classes and workshops for senior citizens
- The increased number of health presentations and related information for senior citizens
- The placement and/or enlargement of computer rooms at Senior Citizen Centers

- The offering of computer classes to senior citizens in these computer rooms at Senior Citizen Centers
- Social Service Workers are being hired to work at Senior Citizen Centers to provide information about the availability of social services to senior citizens

Planning and Building Services

- Some planning services may be obtained from online land-use and zoning information
- Many routine building permits can now be applied for and paid for online
- Zoning maps and property assessment information are frequently available online
- Nationally, there has been some consolidation by state and provincial governments in the number of planning agencies (including local and regional ones)
- Public officials are increasingly taking measures to restore nature on their city's main streets such as narrower streets, wider sidewalks, more trees, an increased number of bushes where trees can't be planted, and benches for citizens to relax – not just to catch the bus

Police Services

- The increased usage of computers in police vehicles (e.g., to obtain citizen information, outstanding warrants, and criminal records) make this information available instantly
- These computer data bases are available at the main department and are continually being updated to provide this information to their law enforcement employees
- There has been an increased number of security programs and services at public schools
- The number of anti-drug educational programs and services for young people at public schools has been increasing
- The increased use of video cameras for surveillance of municipal assets and public spaces to reduce vandalism is now commonplace.
- Many departments are using video cameras to enhance traffic enforcement, such as vehicles running red lights, speeding on public roadways, and related violations

Public Works Services

- The increased usage of GPS (Global Positioning Systems) during inclement weather conditions to properly respond to storms, snow falls, to avoid potential water damage, and to improve driving conditions for citizens
- The use of sophisticated computer software for ongoing vehicle maintenance and vehicle assignments
- Maps showing high traffic accident locations are now frequently available online
- The increased use of online services enables citizens to report things such as the location of graffiti and/or pot holes, which their city can remove and repair promptly

- The increased use of state purchasing contracts to purchase salt, sand, and public works equipment
- Many municipalities are increasingly sharing their specialized equipment for snow melting, pot-hole filling, and the cleaning public streets with neighboring communities

The Future

Public officials and local government employees have almost no control over the dynamics of their "working environment." Societal factors that directly influence the types and levels of the public services that they provide include their political, economic, social, and legal environments. The political environment includes the election of liberals, conservatives, or some combination thereof, which may change over time. The economic environment primarily includes hard-times, good-times, and everything in between, which they have little control over. The social environment includes the impact of an aging population, income levels, educational levels, and unemployment rates, on a community's service levels. Lastly, the elected and appointed officials in municipal government have only limited control over their legal environment, which is primarily set by higher levels of government, and their respective court systems.

Local public officials, both elected and appointed, must respond to these societal changes, but they generally have little or no direct control over them. Frequently, local public officials respond to these societal changes because they have to politically and/or economically. The societal changes taking place in Canada and the United States also directly influence state/provincial and federal officials, and the types and levels of public services that they provide to "their" citizens.

The various levels of government in Canada and the United States are evolving, and their public services are being influenced and impacted by these societal changes. After all, the levels of government must adapt to the societal changes that are taking place in our society, so that they can change the level and quality of the services that they provide to meet the needs, preferences, and demands of the citizens that they serve.

APPENDICES

A. What Governments Do!

Roger L. Kemp, PhD

I. **Taxes**

- Approve New taxes
- Lower existing taxes
- Raise existing taxes
- Leave existing taxes alone

II. **User Fees and Charges**

- Approve New user fee or charge for service
- Lower existing user fee or charge for service
- Raise existing user fee or charge for service
- Leave existing user fee or charge alone

III. **Regulations**

- Approve New regulations
- Lower existing regulations
- Increase existing regulations
- Leave existing regulations alone

IV. **Subsidies and Grants**

- Approve New subsidies and/or grants
- Lower existing subsidies and/or grants
- Increase existing subsidies and/or grants
- Leave existing subsidies and/or grants alone

V. **Public Services**

- Approve New services
- Lower existing services
- Increase existing services
- Leave existing services alone

VI.   **Public Information**

- Provide New information
- Lower existing information
- Increase existing information
- Leave existing information alone

VII.   **Laws**

- Approve New laws
- Modify existing laws
- Leave existing laws alone

VIII.   **Education**

- Approve New educational programs
- Modify existing educational programs
- Leave existing educational programs alone

IX.   **Consultation**

- Approve New consultation programs
- Lower existing consultation programs
- Increase existing consultation programs
- Leave existing consultation programs alone

X.   **Options to Study Problems**

- Direct the staff
- Refer to an existing board or commission
- Create a "study group"
- Form a subcommittee
- Hire a consultant

B. Glossary of Terms

Roger L. Kemp, PhD

Following is a list of terms commonly used to describe city, county, regional, state, and federal governments, and the actions taken by their public officials.

Abolish To do away with; to put an end to.

Act Legislation which has passed both Houses of Congress, approved by the President, or passed over his veto thus becoming law. Also used technically for a bill that has been passed by one House and engrossed.

Adjourn To stop or interrupt a meeting or session for a certain length of time.

Amendment A proposal by a Member (in committee or floor session of the respective Chamber) to alter the language or provisions of a bill or act. It is voted on in the same manner as a bill.

Appeal A request for a new hearing with a higher court.

Appellate Court A court which has the power to hear appeals and reverse court decisions.

Appointed Officials Public officials appointed by elected officials. These officials typically include an organization's top management staff (that is, chief executive and department managers).

Appointment An office or position for which one is chosen, not elected.

Appropriation A formal approval to draw funds from the Treasury for specific purposes. This may occur through an annual appropriations act, an urgent or supplemental appropriations act, a continuing resolution, or a permanent basis.

At-large Elections An election system where candidates are elected on a city-wide basis.

Authorization A law creating or sustaining a program, delegating power to implement it, and outlining its funding. Following authorization, an appropriation actually draws funds from the Treasury.

Bill A proposed law which is being considered for approval.

Bipartisanship Cooperation between Members of both political parties in addressing a particular issue or proposal. Bipartisan action usually results when party leaders agree that an issue is of sufficient national importance as to preclude normal considerations of partisan advantage.

Board of Supervisors Typical name for the members of a governing body of county.

Boards of Commissions Typical names given to advisory bodies, appointed by the members of a governing body, to advise them on matters of importance in one of the many functional areas of government.

Calendar A list of bills, resolutions, or other matters to be considered before committees or on the floor of either House of Congress.

Campaign An attempt to convince people to vote for someone for public office.

Candidate A person seeking to obtain an office or position.

Census An official count of the population.

Charter A written grant which establishes a local government corporation or other institution, and defines its purposes and privileges.

Checks and Balances System of government which maintains balance of power among the branches of the government. Sets limits on the power of each branch. Sets up ways for each branch to correct any misuses of power by the other branches.

Citizen Participation Strategies have greater legitimacy and are easier to implement politically when the citizens served by a governmental entity feel that their interests and issues have been properly addressed during the planning process.

City Council Typical name for the members of a governing body of a municipality.

City Manager The Chief Executive Officer of a municipality.

Civil Relating to the rights of individuals, such as property and personal freedoms. Also, court cases which are not criminal.

Civil Rights Rights which belong to a person because of his or her being a member of a particular society, for example, an American.

Combination Elections A hybrid election system where some candidates are elected on a city-wide basis, while other candidates are elected from a district, or ward.

Committee A group of people officially chosen to investigate or discuss a particular issue.

Compromise To settle differences by accepting less than what was wanted.

Constraint Limitation; restriction.

Contradict To conflict with; to oppose.

Controversial Relating to issues about which people have and express opposing views.

Cost/Benefit Analysis The relationship between economic benefits and cost associated with the operation of the department or program under study. The cost/benefit analysis may include both direct and indirect benefits and costs. Such analysis typically result in a payback period on initial investment.

Cost Center The smallest practical breakdown of expenditure and income into a grouping which will facilitate performance review, service evaluation, and the setting of priorities for particular activity or service area. Typically, it includes apportion of a single program within a department.

County Manager The Chief Executive Officer of a county government.

Cross Impact Analysis An analytical technique for identifying the various impacts of specific events or well-defined policy actions on other events. It explores whether the occurrence of one event or implementation of one policy is likely to inhibit, enhance, or have no effect on the occurrence of another event.

Criminal Relating to court cases in which a person has been accused of committing an action that is harmful to the public, such as murder or burglary.

Debate To discuss reasons for and against an issue or idea.

Delegate To grant or assign responsibility to another; to authorize a person or persons to represent the rest of the people.

Direct Democracy The people vote to make all of the decisions about their government.

Discrimination Being treated differently, usually worse, for some characteristic such as race, religion, national origin or sex. Discrimination is discouraged in the U.S.

District Elections An election system where candidates are elected from a district, or ward.

Econometric Model Forecasting technique that involves a system of interdependent regression equations that describe some sector of economic sales or profit activity. The parameters of the regression equations are usually estimated simultaneously. This technique better expresses the casualties involved than an ordinary regression equation.

Effectiveness Performing the right tasks correctly, consistent with a program's mission, goals, and objectives, or work plan. Relates to correctness and accuracy, not the efficiency of the program or tasks performed. Effectiveness alone is not an accurate measure of total productivity.

Efficiency Operating a program or performing work task economically. Relates to dollars spent or saved, not to the effectiveness of the program or task performed. Efficiency alone is not an accurate measure of total productivity.

Elected Officials Those public officials that hold elective office for a specified time period, typically called a term of office.

Environmental Scanning Process of identifying major environmental factors, events, or trends that impact, directly or indirectly, the organization and its internal operating systems. It is one of the initial steps in undertaking a strategic planning process.

Evaluation Systematic review of the mission, goals, objectives, and work plan for the organization and its various components. Evaluation occurs most frequently at the operational level by reviewing organizational objectives. The evaluation process typically results in the preparation of recommendation for needed adjustments.

Executive Person or group of persons responsible for governmental affairs and enforcement of laws.

Executive Director The title frequently used for the Chief Executive Officer of a regional government agency.

Exempt Free or excused from a requirement or duty.

External Environment All relevant elements or forces (for example, social, economic, political, and technological) external to, and having an impact on, the organization and its various components. Includes those forces that are not under the direct control of management.

Forecasting Techniques Methods (for example, qualitative, quantitative, and causal) used to project trends and predict future events or courses of action. Forecasting is an essential component of the strategic planning process. It may be used to analyze the external environment or to project organizational capabilities.

Foreign Policy The way a country treats and relates to the other countries of the world.

Forms of County Government Major forms include Commission, Commission-Administrator, and Council-Executive.

Forms of Municipal Government Major forms include Council-Manager, Mayor-Council, Commission, and Strong Mayor.

General Election A voting process involving most or all areas of the nation or state.

General Purpose Local Governments Includes cities and counties, since they both provide a wide range of services to the citizens they serve.

Gerrymandering Drawing of district lines to maximize the electoral advantage of political party or faction. The term was first used in 1812, when Elbridge Gerry was Governor of Massachusetts, to characterize the State redistricting plan.

Governor The Chief Executive Officer of a state government.

Hierarchical Ordered by rank or authority.

Hierarchy The order in which authority is ranked.

Impeach To charge a public official with committing a crime.

Inaugurate To place in office by a formal ceremony.

Influence The power to produce or cause an effect; to have an effect upon.

Inherent Rights Essential, basic rights.

Intergovernmental Relations The relationships between public officials at the various levels of government, most often dictated by legislation (e.g., grant requirements).

Internal Environment Relevant elements or forces (e.g., personnel, financial, communications, authority relationships, and management operating systems) internal to, and having an impact on, the operation of the organization and its various components. Includes those forces that are under the direct control of management.

Issue Trend, set of elements, or event which a group decides is important for policy-making purposes.

Issues Management Attempt to manage those issues that are important to an organization. These issues typically surface after the completion of an environmental scanning process, or other practice, leading to the identification of important issues. The issues identified should fall within the scope and purpose of the organization.

Jury A group of people chosen to hear a case in court. The *jury* makes a decision based upon the evidence.

Lame Duck Session A session of Congress meeting after elections have been held, but before the newly elected Congress has convened.

Law In municipal and county government this takes the form of an ordinance, which must be passed by majority vote of the governing body and published in a newspaper of general circulation.

Legislation The act or procedure of making laws; a law or laws made by such a procedure.

Levy To collect, a tax, for example.

Life-Cycle Analysis Involves an analysis and forecasting of new product or service growth rates based on S-curves. The phases of product or service acceptance by various groups are central to this analytical technique.

Line Personnel in those departments charged with responsibility for those functions necessary for the day-to-day performance of the organization. Includes those departments that directly produce goods and/or services to satisfy an organization's marketplace.

Line of Succession Order to succession.

Long-Range Planning Includes a planning process that commences with analyzing the internal organization and projecting current trends into the future for selected organizational components. This planning process may not include an assessment of an organization's external environment. It may be product or service oriented. This term should not be confused with strategic planning.

Management Consists basically of two types—strategic and operational. Strategic management is performed at the top of an organization's hierarchy; everything else is operational management. Operational management is organized along functional lines of responsibility. Strategic management sets direction for the organization, and operational management ensures that this direction is implemented.

Management Information System Integrated information system designed to provide strategic, tactical, and operational information to management. Usually involves periodic written or computer-generated reports which are timely, concise, and meaningful.

Management Operating System Formal system of linkages between different components of the organization by which the various departments communicate with each other and by which management directs the operation and receives information on its performance.

Mayor Typical name for the highest elective office in municipality.

Mission Statement of the role, or purpose, by which an organization plans to serve society. Mission statements may be set for different organizational components or departments. A department usually has only one mission statement.

Municipal The smallest unit of local government in the U.S.

Negotiate To discuss and then compromise on an issue to reach an agreement.

Nonprofit Organization Sometimes referred to as the third sector–the other two being the public and private sectors. Nonprofit organizations generally serve a public purpose and do not generate revenues beyond their operating expenses.

Objectives Tasks which are deemed necessary for an organization, or its components and departments, to achieve its goals. Several detailed objectives are typically set forth for each goal statement. Objectives include the operational implementation of goals.

Operational Issues Issues that relate to the internal operations of an organization such as finance, budgeting, personnel, and technology, to name a few. Operational issues may or may not relate to an organization's external environment and may not be of strategic importance to an organization.

Operational Management Tasks performed by line managers dealing with the operations of the organization. Operational managers may provide input into the formulation of strategic plans, but such plans are formulated by the planning group. Operational managers are key actors in implementing components of strategic plans.

Opponent Person who ran against others in an election for an office or position.

Opportunity Cost Cost of not taking a particular course of action. For example, if there are two issues and one is deemed to be strategic and the other is not, then the opportunity cost is the cost of not pursuing the course of action required for the nonstrategic issue. If the purchase of computers is a strategic issue, and the cost to purchase typewriters is not, then the cost of not acquiring the typewriters is an opportunity cost.

Override To nullify; to pass over.

Pardon To forgive a person for something he/she did wrong; to release or free a person from punishment.

Petition A formal request, usually written, for a right or benefit from a person or group with authority.

Philosophy The general beliefs, attitudes and ideas or theories of a person or group.

Platform The stated principles of a candidate for public office or a political party.

Policy Chosen course of action designed to significantly affect the organization's behavior in prescribed situations.

Political Action Committee (PAC) A group organized to promote its members' views on selected issues, usually through raising money that is contributed to the campaign funds of candidates who support the group's position.

President The Chief Executive Officer of the federal government organization.

Productivity Measure of performance that includes the requirements of both efficiency and effectiveness. Includes performing the program or work tasks correctly (effectively) and economically (efficiently).

Pro Tempore For the time being; temporarily.

Preliminary Introductory; something that comes before and is necessary to what follows.

Preside To hold the position of authority; to be in charge of a meeting or group.

Primary Election Election by which the candidate who will represent a particular political party is chosen.

Ratification Two uses of this term are: (1) the act of approval of a proposed constitutional amendment by the legislatures of the States; (2) the Senate process of advice and consent to treaties negotiated by the President.

Ratify To approve or confirm formally; to make valid and binding.

Redistricting The process within the States of redrawing legislative district boundaries to reflect population changes following the decennial census.

Regional Government A multi-jurisdictional agency that includes any combination of cities and counties, and is usually sub-state in nature. Only a few regional governments involve more than one state.

Regulation Rule or order which controls actions and procedures.

Repeal To take back or recall, usually a law.

Representative Democracy The people choose or elect officials to make decisions for them about their government. On some issues, however, the people vote, rather than their representatives.

Republican Democratic; representative.

Resolution A legislative act without the force of law, such as action taken to adopt a policy or to modify an existing program.

Ruling The official decision of a court on the case being tried.

Sentence Judgment or decision; usually a decision on the punishment for a person convicted of a crime.

Special Purpose Local Governments Includes special districts, which perform a single public service or function (e.g., water, sewer, and transportation districts, to name a few).

Staff Personnel in those departments designed to serve the operating components, or line departments, of an organization (e.g., personnel, finance, general services, purchasing, etc.).

Stakeholder Those individuals, groups, and outside parties that either affect or who are affected by the organization. Examples include constituents, special-interest groups, suppliers, unions, employees, policy-makers, and advisory bodies, to name a few. In any strategic planning process these entities must either be involved or consulted so that their views are given consideration during the planning process.

Strategic Issues Issues included in a strategic plan which are deemed important to the organization and its future performance. These issues may be either internal or external to the organization itself. Typically, external issues are more difficult to manage than internal issues, due to the limited degree of control exercised by public organizations over their outside environment.

Strategic Management Involves setting direction for the organization and typically performed by elected and appointed officials, or some combination of these individuals, once a strategic plan is approved for implementation. While the strategic plan is approved by elected officials, top management is responsible for its administrative implementation.

Strategic Vision Explicit, shared understanding of the nature and purpose of the organization. It specifies what the organization is and should be rather than what it does operationally. The strategic vision is contained within an organization's strategy statement.

Strategy General direction set for the organization and its various components to achieve a desired state in the future. Strategy results from the detailed planning process that assesses the external and internal environment of an organization and results in a work plan that includes mission statements to direct the goals and objectives of the organization.

Structure Segmentation of work into components, typically organized around those goods and services produced, the formal lines of authority and communication between these components, and the information that flows between these communication and authority relationships.

Succession Order in which one person follows another in replacing a person in an office or position.

Table To postpone or delay making a decision on an issue or law.

Time Horizon A timespan included in a plan, or planning document, varies depending on the type of plan being developed. Strategic plans typically have a five or ten year, sometimes longer, time horizon. Operational plans, on the other hand, frequently project a three to five-year timespan into the future.

Unconstitutional In conflict with a constitution.

Veto Power of the head of the executive branch to keep a bill from becoming law.

Editor's Note: Some of the above terms were taken from *U.S. Government Structure* (1987), and *Our American Government* (1993), U.S. Government Printing Office, Washington, D.C. copies of these books may be obtained from the U.S. Government Printing Office, P.O. Box 371954, Pittsburgh, Pennsylvania 15250-7954, or may be ordered over the internet from GPO's online bookstore (http://bookstore.gpo.gov).

C. Local Government Historical Document

(Mecklenburg County was the first local government in America to declare its Independence from Great Britain)

The Mecklenburg Resolution[1]
(May 20, 1775)

I. *Resolved*: That whosoever directly or indirectly abets, or in any way, form, or manner countenances the unchartered and dangerous invasion of our rights, as claimed by Great Britain, is an enemy to this country–to America–and to the inherent and inalienable rights of man.

II. *Resolved*: That we do hereby declare ourselves a free and independent people; are, and of right ought to be a sovereign and self-governing association, under the control of no power, other than that of our God and the General Government of the Congress: To the maintenance of which Independence was solemnly pledge to each other our mutual co-operation, our Lives, our Fortunes, and our most Sacred Honor.

III. *Resolved*: That as we acknowledge the existence and control of no law or legal officer, civil or military, within this county, we do hereby ordain and adopt as a rule of life, all, each, and every one of our former laws, wherein, nevertheless, the Crown of Great Britain never can be considered as holding rights, privileges, or authorities therein.

IV. *Resolved*: That all, each, and every Military Officer in this country is hereby reinstated in his former command and authority, he acting to their regulations, and that every Member present of this Delegation, shall henceforth be a Civil Officer, viz: a Justice of the Peace, in the character of a Committee Man, to issue process, hear and determine all matters of controversy, according to said adopted laws, and to preserve Peace, Union, and Harmony in said county, to use every exertion to spread the Love of Country and Fire of Freedom throughout America, until a more general and organized government be established in this Province

ABRAHAM ALEXANDER, *chairman.*
JOHN MCKNITT ALEXANDER, *Secretary*

REFERENCE

[1] This declaration of independence (with supplementary set of resolutions establishing a form of government) was adopted (as it is claimed) by a convention of delegates from different sections of Mecklenburg County, which assembled at Charlotte May 20, 1775.

D. United States Voting Rights History

Roger L. Kemp, PhD

Year Approved	Title of Decision	A Description of the Voting Rights Decision
1776	Declaration of Independence	The right to vote was approved, but restricted to property owners during the colonial and Revolutionary period during the formation of our new nation.
1787	United States Constitution	States were given the power by the central government to regular their own respective state's voting rights for their citizens.
1856	State Legislation	The State of North Carolina is the last state in the nation to remove property ownership as a legal requirement for voting.
1868	14th Amendment to the U. S. Constitution	Citizenship is graned to all former slaves in states throughout the nation. Voters were still dedfined as male, and voting regulations were still a right of each state.
1870	15th Amendment to the U. S. Constitution	The law was adopted that the right to vote can not be denied by the federal or state governmens based on race.
1887	Daws Act	Citizenship is granted to all native Americans who gave up their respective tribal affiliations.
1890	State Constitution	Wyoming is admitted to statehood and becomes the first state to legislate voting rights for women in its state constitution.
1913	17th Amendment to the U. S. Constitution	New law that allows citizens to vote for members of the U. S. Senate, instead of the past practice of having them elected by State Legislatures.
1915	U. S. Supreme Court Decision	The U. S. Supreme Court outlawed, in Guinn v. United States (Oklahoma), literacy tests for federal elections. The court Ruled that this practice was in violation of the 15th Amendment to the U. S. Constitution.

1920	19th Amendment to the U. S. Constitution	Women were given the right to vote in both state and federal elections.
1924	Indian Citizenship	This law granted all Native Americans the rights of citizenship, including the right to vote in federal elections.
1944	U. S. Supreme Court Decision	The U. S. Supreme court outlawed, in Smith v. Allright (Texas), "white primaries" in Texas and other States. The court rules that this practice was in violation of the 15th Amendment to the U. S. Constitution.
1957	Civil Rights Act	The first law to implement the 15th Amendment to the U. S. Constitution is passed. This law established the Civil Rights Commission, which formally investigates complaints of Voter Discrimination made by citizens.
1960	U. S. Supreme Court Decision	The U. S. Supreme Court. in Gomillion v. Lightfood (Alabama), outlawed the use of "gerrymandering" in election practices. This practice includes boundary determination (or Redistricting) changes being made for electoral damage.
1961	23rd Amendment to the U. S. Constitution	Citizens of Washington, D.C. are given the right to vote in presidential elections.
1964	24th Amendment to the U. S. Constitution	The right for citizens to vote in federal elections cannot be denied for failure to pay a poll tax.
1965	Voting Rights Laws	This law forbids states from imposing discriminatory restrictions on the voting rights of citizens, and provides mechanisms to the federal government for the enforcement of this law. This Act was expanded and renewed in 1970, 1975, 1982, and 2006.
1966	U. S. Supreme Cout Decision	The U. S. Supreme Court, in Harper v. Virginia Board of Education, eliminated the poll tax as a qualification for voting in any election. This practice was found to be in violation of the 24th Amendment to the U. S. Constitution.
1966	U. S. Supreme Court Decision	The U. S. Supreme Court, in South Carolina v. Katzenbach (South Carolina), upheld the legality of the Voting Rights Act of 1965.

1970	Voting Rights Act Amendment	Extended the provisions of the Voting Rights Act for five (5) years. Made the act applicable to areas where less than 50 percent of the eligible voting age population was registered as of November 1968.
1972	U. S. Supreme Court Decision	The U. S. Supreme Court, in Dunn v. Blumstein (Tennessee), ruled that lengthy residency requirements for voting in state and local elections are unconstitutional, and suggested a 30-day Residency period as being adequate.
1975	U. S. Supreme Court Decision	The U. S. Supreme Court, in Oregon v. Mitchell (Oregon), upheld the ban on the use of literacy tests as a requirement for voting. This ban was made permanent in the 1975 Amendments to the Voting Rights Act.
1975	Voting Rights Act Amendments	Extended the provisions of the Voting Rights Act of 1965 for several (7) years. It established coverage for other minority groups, including Native Americans, Hispanic Americans, and Asian Americans. This law also permanently banned literacy tests for the right to vote.
1975	Voting Rights Act Amendments	Mandated that certain voting materials must be printed in languages besides English so that people who do not read English can participate in the voting process.
1982	Voting Rights Act Amendment	This law extended the Voting Rights Act of 1965 for twenty-five (25) years. It allowed jurisdictions that could provide evidence of maintaining a clean voting rights record for at least ten (10) years, to avoid preclearance coverage. Provided for and give instruction to disabled or illiterate voters. Provided for bilingual election materials in jurisdictions with large minority populations.
1984	Voting Rights Act Amendment	Protections for elderly and disabled voters were added to the Voting Rights Act. The Voting Accessibility for the Elderly and Handicapped Act requires states to take specific steps to make the voting process accessible to prople with disabilities.
1992	The Voting Rights Language Assistance Act	This law maintained language assistance for selected language minority populations. It also offered coveage for jurisdictions with significant populations (including Latinos, Asian Americans, and American Indians), who had not been offered language assistance under previous federal mandates.

1993	National Voter Registration Act	Attempts to increase the number of eligible citizens who register to vote by making registration available in each state's Department of Motor Vehicles, as well as public assistance and disabilities agencies.
2002	Help America Vote Act	Law requires that states comply with federal mandates for Provisional ballots; disability access; centralized, computerized voting lists; electronic voting; and the requirements that first-time voters present identification before they can vote.
2003	Federal Voting Standards And Procedures Act	Requires all states to streamline their voter registration process, voting practices, and election procedures.
2006	Voting Rights Act of 2006	Extended the provisions of the Voting Rights Act of 1965 for 25 years. Extended the bilingual election requirements through August 5, 2032. Directed the U. S. Comptroller General to study and report to Congress on the implementation, effectiveness, and efficiency of bilingual voting materials requirements.

E. United States Civil Rights History

Roger L. Kemp, PhD

Year Approved	Title of Decision	A Description of the Civil Rights Decision
1865	13th Amendment to the U. S. Constitution	This law, passed by the 39th Congress, abolished slaveryland involuntary servitude, except as punishment for a crime.
1866	Civil Rights Act	Extended the rights of emancipated slaves by stating that anyone born in the United States regardless of their race is a U. S. citizen.
1870	15th Amendment to the U. S. Constitution	This amendment made it against the law for any state to deprive any citizen of his vote because of race, color, or previous conditions of servitude.
1870/71	Enforcement Acts	The U. S. Congress adopted laws that protected African Americans' right to vote, to hold public office, to serve on juries, and to receive equal protection of federal and state laws.
1871	Civil Rights Act	This national law prohibited race-based violence against African Americans.
1875	Civil Rights Act	This law prohibited discrimination in "public accommodations," which was found to be unconstitutional in 1883.
1954	U. S. Supreme Court Decision	A U. S. Supreme Court decision, Brown v. Board of Education (Topeka, Kansaa), made state laws that established racial segregation in public schools unconstitutional (against the law).
1957	Civil Rights Act	Formed the National Civil Rights Commission.
1959	Unruh Civil Rights Law	A State of California law that prohibits discrimination against minorities in public housing.

1960	Civil Rights Act	Congress established a federal inspection law of local public voter registration polls. It also extended the Civil Rights Commission, and requied states to keep federal voting and registration records from all federal elections.
1964	Civil Rights Act	This national law prohibited discrimination based on sex, as well as color and race, and included religion, national origin, disability, and age, in hiring, promotions, and firing.
1968	Civil Rights Act	Congress prohibited discrimination based on race, color, religion, sex, and national origin by federal and state governments.
1968	Fair Housing Act	Prohibited the discrimination in the sale or rental of approximately 80 percent of the housing in the United States. Prohibited state governments and Native-American tribal governments from violating the constitutional rights of Native Americans.
1987	Civil Rights Restoration Act	Established that anti-discrimination laws are applicable to an entire organization if any part of that organization receives federal funds.
1988	Fair Housing Act	Strengthened the powers of enforcement granted to the Housing and Urban Development Department.
1990	Civil Rights Act	A bill that would have made it easier for plaintiffs to win civil rights cases was vetoed by the President of the United States.
1991	Civil Rights Act	Congress provided the right to a trial by jury on discrimination claims and introduced the possibility of emotional distress damages, while limiting the amount that a jury could award in such cases.
1993	Don't Ask Don't Tell Act	This law prohibited U.S military personnel from discriminating against or harassing closeted gay, lesbian, or bisexual service members or applicants while barring openly gay, lesbian, or bisexual Americans from military service.
1993	Family and Medical Leave Act	This law granted employees the right to take (unpaid) time off from work in order to care for a newborn or recently adopted child or to look after an ill family member.

2009	Fair Pay Act	This law clarified that a discriminatory compensation decision or other practice that is unlawful occurs each time compensation is paid pursuant to the discriminatory compensation decision or other practices and thereby extends the time in which an employee can bring a lawsuit.
2010	Don't Ask Don't Tell Repeal Act	This act allowed openly gay, lesbian, and bisexual Americans to serve without discrimination in the U.S. armed forces.
2013	U.S. v. Windsor (New York)	This law determined that the Defense of Marriage Act's definition of "marriage" and "spouse" as limited to heterosexual unions unconstitutional, thus enabling sam-sex couples to receive "federal benefits."
2014	Schuette v. Coalition to Defend Affirmative Action (Michigan)	This law upheld a State of Michigan Referendum banning the use of affirmative action in student admissions at publicly funded state colleges.
2021	Unruh Civil Rights Act	A California law that prohibits a business from engaging in unlawful discrimination again all persons – their employees as well as their customers.
2021	Tom Bane Civil Rights Act	A new California law that prohibits people from interferring with a person's constitutional rights by force of threat of violene.
2021	Civil Rights Memorial	The State of Alabma approved a state Civil Rights Memorial in the City of Montgomery, Alabama.

F. National Resource Directory

Roger L. Kemp, PhD

(organized by topics for the public, nonprofit, and educational sectors)

Civic Education

Ackerman Center for Democratic Citizenship
(http://www.education.purdue.edu/ackerman-center)

American Democracy Project
(http://www.aascu.org/programs/adp/)

Bill of Rights Institute
(http://www.civiced.org/)

Center for Civic Education
(http://www.civiced.org/)

Center for Youth Citizenship
(http://www.youthcitizenship.org/)

Civic Education Project
(http://www.civiceducationproject.org/)

Civnet
(http://civnet.org/)

Constitutional Rights Foundation
(http://www.crf-usa.org/)

Kellogg Foundation
(http://www.wkkf.org/)

Civic Renewal Initiative
(http://www.ncoc.org/)

National Endowment for Democracy
(http://www.ned.org/)

National Institute for Citizens Education and Law
(https://eric.ed.gov)

Civil Rights and Civil Liberties

American Civil Liberties Union
(http://www.aclu.org/)

Citizens Commission on Civil Rights
(http://www.cccr.org/)

Constitution Society
(http://www.constitution.org/)

Freedom Forum
(http://www.freedomforum.org/)

Judicial Watch
(http://www.judicialwatch.org/)

League of Women Voters
(http://www.lwv.org/)

National Coalition again Censorship
(http://www.ncac.org/)

Project Vote Smart
(http://www.vote-smart.org/)

Historical

Center for the Study of Federalism
(http://www.federalism.org/)

Center for the Study of the Presidency
(http://www.thepresidency.org/)

Constitutional Facts
(http://www.constitutionfacts.com/)

Freedom Foundation at Valley Forge
(http://www.ffvf.org/)

National Constitution Center
(http://www.constitutioncenter.org/)

Supreme Court Historical Society
(http://www.supremecourthistory.org/)

The Avalon Project
(http://avalon.law.yale.edu/)

White House Historical Association
(http://www.whitehousehistory.org/)

Political Parties

Democratic National Committee
(http://www.democrats.org/)

Green Party of North America
(http://www.greens.org/)

Libertarian Party
(http://www.lp.org/)

Natural Law Party
(http://www.natural-law.org/)

Reform Party
(http://www.reformparty.org/)

Republican National Committee
(http://www.gop.com/)

Socialist Party
(http://www.socialist.org/)

Professional Associations

American Bar Association
(http://www.abanet.org/)

American Planning Association
(http://www.planning.org/)

American Political Science Association
(http://www.apsanet.org/)

American Society for Public Administration
(http://www.aspanet.org/)

Association for Metropolitan Planning Organizations
(http://www.ampo.org/)

Public Policy

Association for Public Policy Analysis and Management
(http://www.appam.org/)

Center for Policy Alternatives
(http://www.cfpa.org/)

Center for Public Integrity
(http://www.publicintegrity.org/)

Common Cause
(http://www.commoncause.org/)

National Center for Policy Analysis
(http://www.ncpa.org/)

National Center for Public Policy Research
(http://www.nationalcenter.org/)

National Legal Center for Public Interest
(http://www.nlcpi.org/)

Pew Research Center
(http://pewresearch.org/)

State and Local Government

Council of State Governments
(http://www.csg.org/)

International City/County Management Association
(http://www.icma.org/)

Local Government Commission
(http://www.lgc.org/)

Meyner Center for the Study of State and Local Government
(https://meynercenter.lafayette.edu/)

National Association of Counties
(http://www.naco.org/)

National Association of Regional Councils
(http://www.narc.org/)

National Association of Towns and Townships
(http://natat.org/)

National Center for State Courts
(http://www.ncsc.org/)

National Civic League
(http://www.ncl.org/)

National Conference of State Legislatures
(http://www.ncsl.org/)

National Governors Association
(http://www.nga.org/)

National League of Cities
(http://www.nlc.org/)

Secretary of State/State of Connecticut
(http://www.sots.ct.gov/)

U.S. Conference of Mayors
(http://www.usmayors.org/)

State Supreme Judicial Court Commonwealth of Massachusetts
(http://www.mass.gov/courts/sjcl)

U.S. Government

Federal Communications Commission
(http://www.fcc.gov/)

Federal Elections Commission
(http://www.fec.gov/)

Federal Judicial Center
(http://www.fjc.gov/)

Federal Judiciary Homepage
(http://www.uscourts.gov/)

Library of Congress
(http://lcweb.loc.gov/)

National Endowment for the Humanities
(http://www.neh.gov/)

Thomas Legislative Information
(http://www.congress.gov/)

U.S. Census Bureau
(http://www.census.gov/)

U.S. Department of State
(http://www.state.gov)

U.S. Department of the Interior
(http://www.doi.gov/)

U.S. House of Representatives
(http://www.house.gov/)

U.S. National Archives and Records Administration
(http://www.archives.gov/)

U.S. Senate
(http://www.senate.gov/)

U.S. Supreme Court
(http://www.supremecourtus.gov/)

White House
(http://www.whitehouse.gov/)

Others

Brookings Institution
(http://www.Brookings.edu/)

Civics & The Future of Democracy
(http://futureofcivics.theatlantic.com)

Heritage Foundation
(http://www.heritage.org/)

National Humanities Institute
(http://www.nhinet.org/)

National Taxpayers Union
(http://www.ntu.org/)

National Urban League
(http://www.nul.org/)

Smithsonian Institution
(http://www.si.edu/)

Street Law, Inc.
(http://www.streetlaw.org/)

Supreme Court Decisions
(http://supct.law.cornell.edu/supct/)

United Kingdom Parliamentary Archives
(http://www.parliament.uk/archives/)

Urban Institute
(http://www.urban.org/)

Wikipedia Encyclopedia
(http://www.wikipedia.org/)

NOTE

Some professional association are listed under headings that fit their primary mission. Those that don't fit into one of the general topics are listed above under "others."

G. State Municipal League Directory

Roger L. Kemp, PhD

Most states have a municipal league, which serves as a valuable source of information about city government innovations and programs. Additional information on eminent domain is available from the following state municipal league websites:

Alabama League of Municipalities
(http://www.alalm.org/)

Alaska Municipal League
(http://www.akml.org/)

League of Arizona Cities and Towns
(http://www.azleague.org/)

Arkansas Municipal League
(http://www.arml.org/)

League of California Cities
(http://www.cacities.org/)

Colorado Municipal League
(http://www.cml.org/)

Connecticut Conference of Municipalities
(http://www.ccm-ct.org/)

Delaware League of Local Governments
(http://www.ipa.udel.edu/localgovt/dllg/)

Florida League of Cities
(http://www.flcities.com/)

Georgia Municipal Association
(http://www.gmanet.com/)

Association of Idaho Cities
(http://www.idahocities.org/)

Illinois Municipal League
(http://www.iml.org/)

Indiana Association of Cities and Towns
(http://www.citiesandtowns.org/)

Iowa League of Cities
(http://www.iowaleague.org/)

League of Kansas Municipalities
(http://www.lkm.org/)

Kentucky League of Cities, Inc.
(http://www.klc.org/)

Louisiana Municipal Association
(http://www.lma.org/)

Maine Municipal Association
(http://www.memun.org/)

Maryland Municipal League
(http://www.mdmunicipal.org/)

Massachusetts Municipal Association
(http://www.mma.org/)

Michigan Municipal League
(http://www.mml.org/)

League of Minnesota Cities
(http://www.lmc.org/)

Mississippi Municipal League
(http://www.mmlonline.com/)

Missouri Municipal League
(http://www.mocities.com/)

Montana League of Cities and Towns
(http://www.mtleague.org/)

League of Nebraska Municipalities
(http://www.lonm.org/)

Nevada League of Cities and Municipalities
(http://www.nvleague.org/)

New Hampshire Municipal Association
(http://www.nhmunicipal.org/)

New Jersey State League of Municipalities
(http://www.njlm.org/)

New Mexico Municipal League
(www.nmml.org/))

New York State Conference of Mayors and Municipal Officials
(http://www.nycom.org/)

North Carolina League of Municipalities
(http://www.nclm.org/)

North Dakota League of Cities
(http://www.ndlc.org/)

Ohio Municipal League
(http://www.omlohio.org/)

Oklahoma Municipal League
(http://www.oml.org/)

League of Oregon Cities
(http://www.orcities.org/)

Pennsylvania Municipal League
(http://www.pml.org/)

Rhode Island League of Cities And Towns
(http://www.rileague.org/)

Municipal Association of South Carolina
(http://www.masc.sc/)

South Dakota Municipal League
(http://www.sdmunicipalleague.org/)

Tennessee Municipal League
(http://www.tmll.org/)

Texas Municipal League
(http://www.tml.org/)

Utah League of Cities and Towns
(http://www.ulct.org/)

Vermont League of Cities and Towns
(http://www.vlct.org/)

Virginia Municipal League
(http://www.vml.org/)

Association of Washington Cities
(http://www.awcnet.org/)

West Virginia Municipal League
(http://www.wvml.org/)

League of Wisconsin Municipalities
(http://www.lwm-info.org/)

Wyoming Association of Municipalities
(http://www.wyomuni.org/)

H. State Library Directory

Roger L. Kemp, PhD

Most state libraries have copies of state laws, both proposed and adopted in an on-line database. Many states also have copies of the various laws adopted in those cities and towns within their jurisdictions. They are an excellent resource for eminent domain.

Alabama
Alabama Department of Archives & History,
(http://archives.state.al.us/)

Alabama Public Library Services
(http://statelibrary.alabama.gov/)

Alaska
Alaska State Library
(http://www.library.alaska.gov/)

Arizona
Arizona Department of Library, Archives and Public Records
(http://www.azlibrary.gov/)

Arkansas
Arkansas State Library
(http://www.asl.lib.ar.us/)

California
California State Library
(http://www.library.ca.gov/)

Colorado
Colorado State Library and Adult Education Office
(http://www.cde.state.co.us/cdelib/)

Colorado Virtual Library
(http://www.coloradovirtuallibrary.org/)

Connecticut
Connecticut State Library
(http://www.ctstatelibrary.org/)

Delaware
Delaware Library Catalog Consortium
(https://lib.de.us/about-us/about-dlc/)

Delaware Division of Libraries
(http://www.libraries.delaware.gov/)

District of Columbia
District of Columbia Public Library
(http://www.dclibrary.org/)

Florida
State Library and Archives of Florida
(http://www.dos.myflorida.com/library-archives)

Georgia
Office of Public Library Services
(http://www.georgialibraries.org/)

Hawaii
Hawaii State Public Library System
(http://www.librarieshawaii.org/)

Idaho
Idaho Commission for Libraries
(http://libraries.idaho.gov/)

Illinois
Illinois State Library
(http://www.cyberdriveillinois.com/departments/library)

Indiana
Indiana State Library
(http://www.in.gov/library/)

Iowa
State Library of Iowa
(http://www.statelibraryofiowa.org/)

Kansas
Kansas State Library
(http://www.kslib.info/)

Kentucky
Kentucky Department for Libraries and Archives
(http://www.kdla.ky.gov/)

Louisiana
State Library of Louisiana
(http://www.state.lib.la.us/)

Maine
Maine State Library
(http://www.state.me.us/msl.)

Maryland
Sailor: Maryland's Public Information Network
(http://www.sailor.lib.md.us/)

Massachusetts
Massachusetts Board of Library Commissioners
(http://mblc.state.ma.us/)

Michigan
Library of Michigan
(http://www.michigan.gov/libraryofmichigan)

Minnesota
State Government Libraries
(http://www.libraries.state.mn.us/)

Mississippi
Mississippi Library Commission
(http://www.mlc.lib.ms.us/)

Missouri
Missouri State Library
(http://www.sos.mo.gov/library/)

Montana
Montana State Library
(http://www.home.msl.mt.gov/)

Nebraska
Nebraska Library Commission
(http://www.nlc.state.ne.us/)

Nevada
Nevada State Library and Archives
(http://www.nsladigitalcollections.org)

New Hampshire
New Hampshire State Library
(http://www.nh.gov/nhsl/)

New Jersey
The New Jersey State Library
(http://www.njstatelib.org/)

New Mexico
New Mexico State Library
(http://www.nmstatelibrary.org/)

New York
The New York State Library
(http://www.nysl.nysed.gov/)

New York State Archives
(http://www.archives.nysed.gov/)

North Carolina
State Library of North Carolina
(https://statelibrary.ncder.gov/)

North Dakota
North Dakota State Library
(http://www.library.nd.gov/)

Ohio
State Library of Ohio
(http://www.library.ohio.gov/)

Oklahoma
Oklahoma Department of Libraries
(http://www.odl.state.ok.us/)

Oregon
Oregon State Library
(http://oregon.gov/OSL/)

Pennsylvania
State Library of Pennsylvania
(https://www.statelibrary.pa.gov/)

Rhode Island
Office of Library and Information Services
(http://www.olis.ri.gov/)

South Carolina
South Carolina State Library
(http://www.statelibrary.sc.gov/)

South Dakota
South Dakota State Library
(http://library.sd.gov/)

Tennessee
Tennessee State Library & Archives
(http://www.tennessee.gov/tsla/)

Texas
Texas State Library and Archives Commission
(http://www.tsl.state.tx.us/)

Utah
Utah State Library
(http://library.utah.gov/libraries.vermont.gov/)

Vermont
Vermont Department of Libraries
(http://libraries.vermont.gov/)

Virginia
The Library of Virginia
(http://www.lva.virginia.gov/)

Washington
Washington State Library
(http://www.secstate.wa.gov/library/)

West Virginia
West Virginia Library Commission
(http://wvlc.lib.wv.us/)

West Virginia Archives and History
(http://www.wvculture.org/history/)

Wisconsin
Wisconsin Department of Public Instruction: Division for Libraries, Technology, and Community Learning
(http://www.dpi.wi.gov/dltcl/)

Wyoming
Wyoming State Library
(http://www.library.wyo.gov/)

I. Books by Roger L. Kemp

(as author, contributing author, and editor)

(1) Roger L. Kemp, *Coping with Proposition 13*, Lexington Books, D.C. Heath and Company, Lexington, MA, and Toronto, Canada (1980)

(2) Roger L. Kemp, "The Administration of Scarcity: Managing Government in Hard Times," *Conferencia De Las Ciudades De Las America*, Interamerican Foundation of Cities, San Juan, Puerto Rico (1983)

(3) Roger L. Kemp, *Cutback Management: A Trinational Perspective*, Transaction Books, New Brunswick, NJ, and London, England (1983)

(4) Roger L. Kemp, *Research in Urban Policy: Coping with Urban Austerity*, JAI Press, Inc., Greenwich, CT, and London, England (1985)

(5) Roger L. Kemp, *America's Infrastructure: Problems and Prospects*, The Interstate Printers and Publishers, Danville, IL (1986)

(6) Roger L. Kemp, *Coping with Proposition 13: Strategies for Hard Times*, Robert E. Krieger Publishing Company, Malabar, FL (1988)

(7) Roger L. Kemp, *America's Cities: Strategic Planning for the Future*, The Interstate Printers and Publishers, Danville, IL (1988)

(8) Roger L. Kemp, *The Hidden Wealth of Cities: Policy and Productivity Methods for American Local Governments*, JAI Press, Inc., Greenwich, CT and London, England (1989)

(9) Roger L. Kemp, *Strategic Planning in Local Government: A Casebook*, Planners Press, American Planning Association, Chicago, IL, and Washington, D.C. (1992)

(10) Roger L. Kemp, *Strategic Planning for Local Government*, International City/County Management Association, Washington, D.C. (1993)

(11) Roger L. Kemp, *America's Cities: Problems and Prospects*, Avebury Press, Alershot, England (1995)

(12) Roger L. Kemp, *Helping Business – The Library's Role in Community Economic Development, A How-To-Do-It Manual*, Neal-Schuman Publishers, Inc., New York, NY, and London, England (1997)

(13) Roger L. Kemp, *Homeland Security: Best Practices for Local Government*, 1st Edition, International City/County Management Association, Washington, D.C. (2003)

(14) Roger L. Kemp, *Cities and the Arts: A Handbook for Renewal*, McFarland & Company, Inc., Jefferson, NC (2004)

(15) Roger L. Kemp, *Homeland Security Handbook for Citizen and Public Officials*, McFarland & Company, Inc., Jefferson, NC (2006)

(16) Roger L. Kemp, *Main Street Renewal: A Handbook for Citizens and Public Officials*, McFarland & Company, Inc., Jefferson, NC (2006, 2000)

(17) Roger L. Kemp, *Local Government Election Practices: A Handbook for Public Officials and Citizens*, McFarland & Company, Inc., Jefferson, NC (2006, 1999)

(18) Roger L. Kemp, *Cities and Nature: A Handbook for Renewal*, McFarland & Company, Inc., Jefferson, NC (2006)

(19) Roger L. Kemp, *Emergency Management and Homeland Security*, International City/County Management Association, Washington, D.C. (2006)

(20) Roger L. Kemp, *The Inner City: A Handbook for Renewal*, McFarland & Company, Inc., Jefferson, NC (2007, 2001)

(21) Roger L. Kemp, *Privatization: The Provision of Public Services by the Private Sector*, McFarland & Company, Inc., Jefferson, NC (2007, 1991)

(22) Roger L. Kemp, *Community Renewal through Municipal Investment: A Handbook for Citizens and Public Officials*, McFarland & Company, Inc., Jefferson, NC (2007, 2003)

(23) Roger L. Kemp, *How American Government Works: A Handbook on City, County, Regional, State, and Federal Operations*, McFarland & Company, Inc., Jefferson, NC (2007, 2002)

(24) Roger L. Kemp, *Regional Government Innovations: A Handbook for Citizens and Public Officials*, McFarland & Company, Inc., Jefferson, NC (2007, 2003)

(25) Roger L. Kemp, *Economic Development in Local Government: A Handbook for Public Officials and Citizens*, McFarland & Company, Inc., Jefferson, NC (2007, 1995)

(26) Roger L. Kemp, *Model Practices for Municipal Governments*, Connecticut Town and City Management Association, University of Connecticut, West Hartford, CT (2007)

(27) Roger L. Kemp, *Managing America's Cities: A Handbook for Local Government Productivity*, McFarland & Company, Inc., Jefferson, NC (2007, 1998)

(28) Roger L. Kemp, *Model Government Charters: A City, County, Regional, State, and Federal Handbook*, McFarland & Company, Inc., Jefferson, NC (2007, 2003)

(29) Roger L. Kemp, *Forms of Local Government: A Handbook on City, County and Regional Options*, McFarland & Company, Inc., Jefferson, NC (2007, 1999)

(30) Roger L. Kemp, *Cities and Cars: A Handbook of Best Practices*, McFarland & Company, Inc., Jefferson, NC (2007)

(31) Roger L. Kemp, *Homeland Security for the Private Sector: A Handbook*, McFarland & Company, Inc., Jefferson, NC (2007)

(32) Roger L. Kemp, *Strategic Planning for Local Government: A Handbook for Officials and Citizens*, McFarland & Company, Inc., Jefferson, NC (2008, 1993)

(33) Roger L. Kemp, *Museums, Libraries and Urban Vitality: A Handbook*, McFarland & Company, Inc., Jefferson, NC (2008)

(34) Roger L. Kemp, *Cities and Growth: A Policy Handbook*, McFarland & Company, Inc., Jefferson, NC (2008)

(35) Roger L. Kemp, *Cities and Sports Stadiums: A Planning Handbook*, McFarland & Company, Inc., Jefferson, NC (2009)

(36) Roger L. Kemp, *Cities and Water: A Handbook for Planning*, McFarland & Company, Inc., Jefferson, NC (2009)

(37) Roger L. Kemp, *Homeland Security: Best Practices for Local Government*, 2nd Edition, International City/County Management Association, Washington, D.C. (2010)

(38) Roger L. Kemp, *Cities and Adult Businesses: A Handbook for Regulatory Planning*, McFarland & Company, Inc., Jefferson, NC (2010)

(39) Roger L. Kemp, *Documents of American Democracy: A Collection of Essential Works*, McFarland & Company, Inc., Jefferson, NC (2010)

(40) Roger L. Kemp, *Strategies and Technologies for a Sustainable Future*, World Future Society, Bethesda, MD (2010)

(41) Roger L. Kemp, *Cities Going Green: A Handbook of Best Practices*, McFarland & Company, Inc., Jefferson, NC (2011)

(42) Roger L. Kemp, *The Municipal Budget Crunch: A Handbook for Professionals*, McFarland & Company, Inc., Jefferson, NC (2012)

(43) Roger L. Kemp, Frank B. Connolly, and Philip K. Schenck, *Local Government in Connecticut*, 3rd Edition, Wesleyan University Press, Middletown, CT (2013)

(44) Roger L. Kemp, *Town and Gown Relations: A Handbook of Best Practices*, McFarland & Company, Inc., Jefferson, NC (2013)

(45) Roger L. Kemp, *Global Models of Urban Planning: Best Practices Outside the United States*, McFarland & Company, Inc., Jefferson, NC (2013)

(46) Roger L. Kemp, *Urban Transportation Innovations Worldwide: A Handbook of Best Practices Outside the United States*, McFarland & Company, Inc., Jefferson, NC (2015)

(47) Roger L. Kemp, *Immigration and America's Cities: A Handbook on Evolving Services*, McFarland & Company, Inc., Jefferson, NC (2016)

(48) Roger L. Kemp, *Corruption and American Cities: Essays and Case Studies in Ethical Accountability*, McFarland & Company, Inc., Jefferson, NC (2016)

(49) Roger L. Kemp, *Privatization in Practice: Reports on Trends, Cases and Debates in Public Service by Business and Nonprofits*, McFarland & Company, Inc., Jefferson, NC (2016)

(50) Roger L. Kemp, *Small Town Economic Development: Reports on Growth Strategies in Practice*, McFarland & Company, Inc., Jefferson, NC (2017)

(51) Roger L. Kemp, Donald F. Norris, Laura Mateczun, Cory Fleming, and Will Fricke, *Cybersecurity: Protecting Local Government Digital Resources*, International City/County Management Association, Washington, D.C. (2017)

(52) Roger L. Kemp, *Eminent Domain and Economic Growth: Perspectives on Benefits, Harms and Trends*, McFarland & Company, Inc., Jefferson, NC (2018)

(53) Roger L. Kemp, *Senior Care and Services: Essays and Case Studies on Practices, Innovations and Challenges*, McFarland & Company, Inc., Jefferson, NC (2019)

(54) Roger L. Kemp, *Cybersecurity: Current Writings on Threats and Protection*, McFarland & Company, Inc., Jefferson, NC (2019)

(55) Roger L. Kemp, *Veteran Care and Services: Essays and Case Studies on Practices, Innovations and Challenges*, McFarland & Company, Inc., Jefferson, NC (2020)

(56) Roger L. Kemp, *Civics 101 – Poems About America's Cities*, Kindle Direct Publishing, Middletown, DE (2020)

(57) Roger L. Kemp, *Civics 102 – Stories About America's Cities*, AuthorHouse Publishing. Bloomington, IN (2021)

(58) Roger L. Kemp, *Civics 103 – Charters that Form America's Governments*, AuthorHouse Publishing. Bloomington, IN (2021)

(59) Roger L. Kemp, *Civics 104 – America's Evolving Boundaries*, AuthorHouse Publishing. Bloomington, IN (2021)

(60) Roger L. Kemp, *Civics 105 – Documents that Formed America*, AuthorHouse Publishing. Bloomington, IN (2021)

(61) Roger L. Kemp, *Civics 106 – Documents that Formed the United Kingdom and the United States*, AuthorHouse Publishing. Bloomington, IN (2021)

J. Presentations by Roger L. Kemp

- American Library Association
- American Management Association
- American Society for Public Administration
- Association of Contingency Planners
- Australian Institute of Municipal Mgmt.
- California League of Women Voters
- Capital Regional Council of Govts.
- Conf. of the Great Cities of the Americas
- Connecticut Bar Association
- Connecticut Conference of Municipalities
- Connecticut Town & City Management Assn.
- European Union
- Government Finance Officers Association
- Institute of Urban & Regional Development
- International City/County Management Assn.
- League of California Cities
- League of Women Voters
- Missouri City/County Management Assn.
- National Public Admin Honor Society
- National Public Library Association
- State of Connecticut
- Texas Public Power Association
- The Writers' Network
- U.S. Chamber of Commerce
- U.S. Department of Homeland Security
- U.S. Department of Justice
- U.S. Presidential Interns
- World Future Society

Printed in the United States
by Baker & Taylor Publisher Services